NO
EXPERTS
NEEDED

NO EXPERTS NEEDED

◆

The Meaning of Life According to *You!*

LOUISE LEWIS

iUniverse, Inc.
New York Lincoln Shanghai

NO EXPERTS NEEDED
The Meaning of Life According to You!

iUniverse books may be ordered through booksellers or by contacting:

iUniverse
2021 Pine Lake Road, Suite 100
Lincoln, NE 68512
www.iuniverse.com
1-800-Authors (1-800-288-4677)

Talking To My Angel
Written by Melissa Etheridge
Copyright © 1999 MLE Music (ASCAP)
All rights reserved. Used by permission.

ISBN: 978-0-595-42971-4 (pbk)
ISBN: 978-0-595-87312-8 (ebk)

Printed in the United States of America

For the generous spirit who supports my every step ...

We shall not cease from exploration
And the end of all our exploring
Will be to arrive where we started
And know the place for the first time.

—T. S. Eliot, "Little Gidding" from *Four Quartets*

Contents

Acknowledgments

It is with heartfelt gratitude that I thank all of my family members and friends for their love and encouragement at every step of my Spirit-driven journey.

I especially want to thank family members Momma (Yvonne Matherne), Diane Seely, Tina Kovaleski, Adam Zelasko, and Ted Zelasko, and friends Susan Hubbard and Cathie Hanson for having the courage to read and give honest feedback on early drafts.

I thank my dear friends Steve Norde, Lisa McGuerrell, and Hugh Lamond for always providing your loving support and guidance.

I thank Melissa Etheridge for the words and music to "Talking to My Angel." Her song walked me through to the other side of my fears about writing and publishing this book.

I humbly thank the grace and spirit of one particular daytime talk-show host for her inspiration and unwavering commitment to make this world a better place. She is a shining example of how I want to love out loud.

Above all else, I thank God for giving me the ability to listen to His words with an open ear, an open mind, and an open heart.

Introduction

I have always believed that everyone has a book in them. They merely have to take a look at their lives, past or present, to realize that life is indeed stranger than fiction. More likely than not, everyone's lives would make for quite an entertaining story, to say the least.

Now I'm not saying that I think everyone's book would be worthy of a Pulitzer or be chosen for Oprah's Book Club. You're holding the evidence to back up that statement on both accounts. But I do think there is something special and unique about each of our lives that should be written down and then shared with others. Having said all of that, I was totally unaware of the book that was lurking deep inside of me. I discovered it (or rather it discovered me) when I unexpectedly began a new chapter in my life.

The story I'm sharing with you began when I was set free (laid off) from my job of eleven years selling advertising space for publications in high tech. Being set free simultaneously marked the beginning of a new chapter in my life. From day one of this new chapter, many truths were revealed to me. For instance, I immediately interpreted being set free from my job as something positive from which I would later benefit, rather than something negative that I would be challenged to overcome. Even though it would've been easy to panic about no longer having a source of income, I chose not to waste any energy thinking about the negative aspect of the situation.

Another truth that revealed itself was the knowledge that I was supposed to take advantage of the rare opportunity of having some time off. Therefore, I didn't immediately start looking for another job. Granted, with no source of income, this was an odd decision to make. However, I had worked nonstop since the age of sixteen, and I felt that I deserved some time away from the rat race. That was my story, and I faithfully stuck to it.

Adding to the list of truths was the fact that I knew, without a doubt, that whatever I experienced during this new chapter of my life would have a profound and lasting effect on my future. Without knowing how or why, I was very aware from the start that I was being lovingly, divinely guided toward something special.

The last of my truths was knowing that the significance of the choices I would make during my new chapter would be revealed to me one at a time, and only when I was in the moment—not a minute sooner.

Armed with these truths, I not only felt excited but also well prepared to begin my new chapter. But no matter how ready I felt, I was acutely aware of the fact that if this indeed was a new chapter, nothing but blank pages stared me in the face. *Where was I to begin?*

After a bit of soul-searching, the one thing I knew for certain was that I wanted my new chapter in life to be based on a commitment to living in Spirit, rather than in Ego.

As I see it, the ego houses the more base elements of human nature, for example, fear, self-doubt, criticism, control issues, and selfishness that if left unchecked, will create negative energy in my life. On the flip side, when my life is focused on Spirit, the ultimate Source of truth, I am guided by more positive elements, such as courage, forgiveness, compassion and generosity.

Therefore, the first step of my journey involved making a commitment to allow Spirit to guide my every move and to let nothing stand in the way of that. I was convinced that by following Spirit, the pages of my new chapter would be filled with a very special story, one that would involve adventure, personal growth, and a change in lifestyle.

As my new chapter developed, my path crossed with those of many wonderful people—normal, everyday folks whom I met during my travels, as well as in my own backyard. I listened to their stories along the way. After each encounter, I asked these people (along with family and friends) for a gift. I asked everyone to answer one question: what is the meaning of life?

I also insisted that each person provide a spontaneous answer. In other words, he or she had to write the answer right then and there, while in my presence. Why did I insist on this? To answer that question, I have to adapt the saying "God lives in the details." My version goes something like this: I believe that God (the ultimate truth) lives in the spontaneous moment. I also believe that what you know to be true can be communicated in the moment, right now, without long deliberation or second-guessing. And you certainly don't need an expert to tell you what you already know.

Not surprisingly, the overwhelming majority of people I met agreed to join in on the adventure of my book. And I walked away from this journey with my heart filled with memorable gifts that will reward me until the end of my days.

Writing this book has been a personal journey for me as well as for some of the people you are about to meet. Due to the personal nature of some of their stories, I am not divulging every detail out of respect for each person. However, I will share with you the fact that with each person I met, I was reminded that I was not alone.

With each meeting, I was reminded that no matter what their race, religion, or geography, people possess far more similarities than they do differences. When you think about it, we all eventually experience pretty much the same stuff that life dishes out: the same joys, the same pain, the same sorrow. Somehow, believing this allows me to walk through life with a greater sense of belonging in the world.

I will forever be grateful to the people I met along the way. Because of them, I'm more committed than ever to being a more curious participant in life, a more compassionate listener, and a more adamant believer in the saying "We are all alike."

I know that I cannot change the whole world, but I most certainly can change *my* world by asking those around me to lay focus to the meaning in their life. Therefore, it is my sincere hope that this book ignites conscious thought so that more people can find their own answers to the meaning of life. With this hope in my heart, I invite you to begin your own journey of discovery, which may very well begin by you asking this question to those people who cross your path. You'll be amazed by what you hear.

And so, the tale of my journey begins. Thank you for coming along!

A Book Is Born

On October 9, 2002, I was "set free" from my job of eleven years, an event more commonly known as getting laid off. Since I'm a nauseatingly positive person most of the time, it was quite natural for me to shine a positive light over losing my job as well. I now know that if it weren't for losing my job, I would not have been in such a vulnerable state of mind; had I not been in such a vulnerable state of mind, I would not have been open to seeing the moment as the start of a new chapter in my life. Ultimately, both worked hand in hand and allowed me to receive help and guidance, which Spirit immediately provided.

Even though I maintained a lighter heart about losing my job than would most people, I don't make light of the impact that getting laid off can have on someone's life. Losing a job can be emotionally as well as financially devastating. However, in my case, getting set free came neither as a shock nor a surprise because my industry had been in trouble for a couple of years.

For two years, I watched as that dreaded pink slip was given to many people around me, clients and co-workers alike. Prior to receiving my own pink slip, I had stated many times that if I had been my own employee, faced with the same economic conditions, I would have laid off myself. Therefore, in hindsight, I think I was as mentally prepared as I could have been.

I knew my time had come to get "pinked" when my boss asked to meet with me the next time I had appointments in her area (Silicon Valley). Even though my Southern California office was only an hour's flight away, my boss had never before called for a face-to-face meeting. Her sudden interest in a meeting alerted me to what was about to happen.

The meeting day arrived. I gingerly entered my boss's office, still holding on to the slightest hope that my intuition was wrong.

"Hi, Louise!" she said, unable to look me in the eye. "You look great. New suit? Lost weight?"

Now, being a normal female with a healthy ego, any other time I would have just accepted her compliments graciously and not thought anymore about it. However, her peppering of compliments only confirmed my suspicions.

"Gee, all of these compliments …" I replied. "Are you laying me off today?"

To say the least, my boss turned pale and appeared rather startled by my remark. *Busted!*

She squeaked out a nervous laugh. "Let's meet in the conference room to talk about your territory."

Talk about my territory? Yeah, right!

The deed was done with much grace and professionalism from both sides of the table. If there was anything good about my exit interview, it was that my boss cried as she recalled my role in her getting a job at our company. I chuckled at the irony of the situation but knew that the emotion filling my heart would soon have to be released. But not here.

When I think back on that moment, I cringe at having delivered such a blunt "psychic" remark that made my former boss feel so uncomfortable. Despite the fact that she was the one to hand me my pink slip, I continue to respect her.

Spirit's First Words

Within minutes of getting set free from my job, I sat at the airport gate and waited for my flight home to Southern California. My fingers automatically dialed for the love of my sister before I even realized I had pulled out my cell phone.

"Dee?" I choked out her name as tears stung my eyes.

Merely speaking her name broke down my defenses.

"What's wrong?" she softly whispered.

"I just got laid off."

Her faint gasp followed by a stretch of silent confusion reflected the numbness of my mind.

"Oh, Lou, I am so sorry," she said.

What else could she say?

"Call Momma," I said. "Let her know."

The mere mention of her name made me want to crawl into Momma's arms and cry until the hurt went away.

Swallowing the huge lump in my throat, I added, "I'll call back when I get home."

Once that was taken care of, I sat at the gate, alone with my thoughts. Or at least I thought I was alone.

Amid the hustle and bustle of the airport, I sat encased in a thick fog that blurred my vision of travelers parading before me. Common airport noises became muffled as they drifted through the haze. The only clear sound I heard was that of my own labored breaths and the frantic thoughts that swirled through my head.

Oh my God, I don't have a job. I have a mortgage! With everyone getting laid off, where will I find a job? How easy it would have been to just lose it and let fear take over.

While I pondered these wild thoughts, I started to visualize myself standing on the edge of a deep crevasse. I looked down into the blackness and saw my toes dangling dangerously over the edge. My body swayed freely in a circular motion.

I toyed with the idea that at any moment, I could choose to lean forward and fall into the long spiral downward, letting myself sink into a deep, dark depression. It may have only lasted for seconds, but the thoughts of falling crept slowly across my mind. Then I fell.

I spiraled down into the black crevasse. The vision of falling played out in my mind as if set in slow motion. And then suddenly, as soon as the vision fully developed in my mind like that of a Polaroid photo, another image emerged. This image was of two cupped hands rising up to meet me (much like the picture of the hands in the old Allstate commercial: "you're in good hands with Allstate").

The closer I came to the hands, the faster I fell. And as my body met with the hands, I plopped down into the safety of God's palms.

The physical sensation of falling was so real that my body actually felt the bounce when I landed in God's hands. In fact, my landing felt so real that it jarred me back to reality and to the bustling airport. I looked around the waiting area to make sure that no one saw me jump in my seat.

Not sure of what had just happened, I took a deep breath and sat quietly as I got back in touch with reality. With more deep breaths, I released all thoughts about the dark crevasse image from my mind and exhaled any negative energy that the image may have caused.

The deep breathing helped quiet my mind. Then I sat in total silence.

What am I going to do? I thought as I lowered my head. Tears broke free.

With my next deep breath, my head was lifted, and through the exhalation of air, I received Spirit's words: *You're going to be OK, Louise. I'll take care of you.*

Hearing those sweet words was all it took for me to release a deluge of pent-up emotions. I was fully aware that I was still sitting in the middle of a busy airport, but I didn't try to control the tears. My cry, complete with full-body sobs and water spewing from every conceivable opening in my head, lasted for several minutes. I cried through feelings of sorrow, relief, and joy, all at the same time.

When the emotion subsided, a warm, healing glow flowed through my entire being. The weight of my worries had suddenly lifted up and out of my body. I felt light. I felt loved. I felt at peace.

After checking to make sure that my mascara was no longer dripping from my face, I took another deep breath and received yet another image. This time it was a beautiful hardcover book, lying open to blank pages. As I looked at the book, my head was once again lifted to hear more of Spirit's words.

This is only a new chapter in your life, He said as if shrugging his shoulders to say, "It's no big deal."

I immediately understood the magnitude of His words, and in that moment, I knew my world was about to change. I knew that my life was already set on a path not of my own creation.

Then, He uttered a life-altering message.

You hold the pen; I'll guide your hand. And together, we'll write one hell of a chapter.

From that day on, God and I have been coauthors of my new chapter.

Each time I replay the events of that day in the airport, I cry. I continue to welcome these tears because I know that they come from gratitude. I'm grateful for everything that had to occur in order for me to experience that unbelievable moment in the airport.

The Conception and the
Oprah Connection

Once I was set free from my job, I decided that I deserved to take some time off to regroup before looking for work. I wanted to experience what life would be like free from the control of a watch or an alarm clock. I also deserved to take advantage of my severance package, thank you very much.

It didn't take long to realize that relaxing at home during the day was far more fun than working. It was no contest: fighting the freeways of Southern California versus reading a good book in the comfort of my own home. Heck, even watching daytime TV was more fun than working. In fact, every day at 3:00 PM I stopped everything to watch one particular program: *Oprah!* One episode in particular really caught my attention.

The day was November 5, 2002, a day I will never forget. The episode was called "What Does the World Think of Us?" In it, Oprah joined forces with CNN reporters around the world to ask people on the street one question: what do you think of Americans? The answers that people gave were very interesting, and I'm sure that episode provided a wake-up call to American viewers as to how we're perceived outside of our borders.

The more I thought about the *Oprah*/CNN episode, the more excited I became about doing something similar. The only thing I had to do was come up with my own question. I didn't think that I'd have a problem with this because I'm *always* asking people thought-provoking questions. One thing you must understand about me is that I'm not one to favor small talk. I can only chitchat with someone for about five minutes, and then I have to take the conversation to deeper levels. So, as I saw it, my biggest dilemma was narrowing the field down to one question. But what question would I take to the streets?

After wrestling with a number of possible scenarios for a few minutes, I quickly gave up, put the entire project out of my mind, and went about my day.

As always, the answer came at the perfect time (in God's time) and was delivered to me on a perfect night ... my birthday.

The Answer Revealed

On November 13, 2002 (only a few weeks after being set free), I treated myself to an elegant dinner at Bayside Restaurant in Newport Beach, California. I was there to celebrate. After all, it was my birthday, and yes, I was alone.

Now to those who don't know me, it may sound pretty pathetic to be celebrating a birthday all alone. Actually, it may even sound pretty sad to those who think they know me best. But thankfully, a few people in my life know that I actually *embrace* moments like these and allow them the freedom to turn into great adventures.

For those of you who just have to know why I was alone, it was because none of my local-yokel friends remembered my birthday. Now *that's* pathetic! Of course, I could have dropped hints to remind them, but I think that would have been tacky to do.

Fortunately, I look back on that birthday and know that had that night played out any differently, my book may never have been conceived. So for that, I guess I have to thank all of those forgetful friends.

I arrived at the restaurant, walked into the bar, and sat down in the "designated" chair. (Even though there were several people sitting at the bar, each person had left exactly two empty chairs between himself and the next person.) Now I ask you: is it not odd that when people put themselves into a social situation, they intentionally distance themselves from others? This continues to baffle me, but there you have it.

I ordered a glass of wine and cracked open my journal.

Remember, at this point in my life, I was unemployed and alone on my birthday. Still sounds pretty pathetic, huh? Not a chance. For it was in this moment that I began one of the biggest adventures of my life.

I quickly filled the pages of my journal with my thoughts, ramblings, and profound recollections. As I flipped to a new page, from my left side I heard a few words tossed my way.

"You shouldn't be working so hard," said the older gentleman nursing his drink.

Of course, having just lost my job, the irony made me giggle.

"Oh, no. It's not work at all," I said with a grin from ear to ear.

It was clear that the tanned-face man was interested in striking up a conversation, and with the exchange of a few pleasantries, I could tell that he was not trying to hit on me.

We enjoyed a few minutes of small talk, but then quickly plunged into deeper conversation about our lives.

Carlos was born in South America and moved to the United States as a young boy. Although he grew up in Pittsburgh, when it came time to find a job, he chose to move to New York City.

"For as long as I can remember," Carlos said, "something inside told me that the American dream was mine for the taking."

A look of determination filled his eyes as he continued, "One day, I walked down Fifth Avenue and pointed to certain buildings. And to each building I said, 'I'm going to work in that building one day. And that one. And that one.'"

Carlos's recollections seemed to take him back in time, and I closely watched his face as his memories paraded before his eyes.

"Even though I had to start at the bottom, in the mailroom, I ended up working in every building that I pointed to that day," he proudly proclaimed.

Although Carlos had been a successful businessperson for some time, he still seemed to look back on his struggles as a youth with much fondness.

The courage and determination of young Carlos was impressive, and while he shared more of his story, I started to imagine what it would be like to put his idea into action in my own life. Just point to what I want in life and then go get it. Point to happiness and claim it. Point to peace and create it. Something like the Nike ads: "Just do it." I liked that idea.

As Carlos launched into another story, something strange started happening to me. My mind began separating into two parts. The front part continued to listen intently to Carlos, while at the same time, the back part began receiving a message from Spirit.

Without any prelude, Spirit began speaking. *You now know what question to ask. And you now know what you have to do.*

And do you know what? I did know! In that moment, I had been given the question that I would begin asking people. I thought back to the inspiration I felt watching that *Oprah* episode. It's funny to think that the *answer* I had been looking for came in the form of a *question*.

The divide in my mind then sealed back together, and I returned my full attention to Carlos. When his story was over, I took a deep breath and declared my mission.

"I am writing a book. And I would like you to be in it," I proclaimed.

The words sounded so odd yet felt so right.

"Yes, yes. Whatever you want," Carlos said as he all but grabbed the pen out of my hand, happy to be the first entry in my book. His eagerness convinced me that he had also felt the unspoken connection and trust we had shared that night.

"I would like you to give me your spontaneous answer to what is the meaning of life?"

As they say, the rest is history.

Carlos

> It is the rational "intent" from a human being to know the universe through knowing himself.

There are many reasons why I will always remember that particular birthday. Receiving Spirit's message sure does top the list. But I will also remember the role that Carlos played that night. I know he was put there to remind me that hidden treasure could always be discovered within the heart of the "stranger" sitting next to me.

Now that I had my question, and my first answer, I knew that my journey had begun. And from the outset, I promised myself to live this adventure to the fullest.

Deliver Us From ...

I felt like I was on some sort of mission, but what kind of mission? Why me? What was I supposed to do now? Sure, I had been given a question to ask people, but what was my next step? I knew I had to keep taking steps that would move me forward down my path, but where was I going?

I didn't have any answers, but I did know that everything was going to be OK. If nothing else, I trusted that. Well, most times.

Standing at this major crossroad in my life scared the poo out of me. And having all of these questions constantly swirling through my head did not help matters much. So when the pressure of these unanswered questions got the better of me (as it did many times along the way), I took out my secret weapon—a song. To fight the fear building inside me, I simply sang along to a Melissa Etheridge song—"Talking to My Angel."

Let me share with you a few of the lyrics to this powerful song ...

Don't be Afraid
Close your eyes
Lay it all down
And don't you cry
Can't you see I'm going
Where I can see the sun rise
I've been talking to my angel
And he said that it's alright

I have yet been able to follow Melissa's advice not to cry. Because whenever I "lay it all down" (which for me means handing over all of my fears and worries to God), that one act combined with the beauty of the song, makes me cry like a baby. And that's a good thing because a good cry always releases the pressure from my body and puts me back on track.

With the memory still fresh of the night I met Carlos and received the first answer to my meaning of life question, I was excited to take more steps on my new journey.

A few days later, with journal and lucky pen in hand, I wandered into Waters Restaurant in Irvine, California, for a bite to eat. It did not take long for my attention to be gently directed toward the man with the curly ponytail standing next to me. He offered his name, Garrett, and asked about my writing. We spoke for only a few minutes when I sensed that he would be a good candidate to answer my meaning of life question.

Garrett

> To do good in the eyes of the Lord. To understand the Abramic covenant. To read the words of the prophets and to read in those words the design of the Lord, the one true God of us all. Then, to understand the renewed covenant that is offered through the Messiah as predicted in Psalm 23 and Isaiah 54 and carried out in the new (covenant) testament gospels of Matthew, Mark, Luke, and John, and further amplified in Romans, Galatians, and Corinthians and particularly recounted in Acts. The sea is water, but not the water of life, which is through Jesus. The boat moves not the sea.

After reading Garrett's answer, I looked deep into his eyes and saw pain, healing, honesty, struggle, and surrender all wrapped up in a clear vision of the Truth. The complexity of emotions I saw in his eyes compelled me to push the envelope and ask one final question.

"Why did you choose to give this particular answer?" I asked.

He lowered his head as he collected his thoughts. "When you are so lost that you are absolutely sure no one would ever forgive you under any circumstances, when you have given up all hope of finding any love, when you have come to the absolute point of no further hope, when you know no one will ever love you, don't ever forget the one who promises to do so."

The beauty and sincerity of Garrett's words touched my soul, and I cried. Actually, I have cried almost every time I have read his response.

As I look back, it still remains a struggle for me to properly articulate the effect Garrett and his words had on me that night. Maybe knowing the proper words is not as important as remembering the feeling. For in that brief meeting, I felt as though I had been given the privilege of seeing a glimpse into Garrett's life … a life that most likely created the passion behind his answer.

I know that Garrett's words will touch many lives and help others find their way to the Light, the same Light that heals the darkness hidden within us all.

I left the restaurant that evening feeling amazed by what had transpired. What began as a seemingly ordinary event of striking up a conversation with a stranger, turned into a beautiful moment filled with trust, openness and truth. Who was it who said, "Beauty is truth, truth beauty"?

A Tropical Paradise

To kick off the celebration of my unemployed life, I traveled to the Big Island of Hawaii to serve as the maid of honor in a friend's wedding.

It is no wonder that so many weddings take place in Hawaii, because the scent of romance is always in the air and the islands' natural beauty make for a perfect setting. A glorious crimson sunset served as the backdrop to my friend's ceremony, while crashing waves of the Pacific sang the melody of the islands.

How romantic and how *fun* it is to be at a wedding alone!

When I attend a wedding or other intimate gathering of friends and family, I am able to mentally remove myself from the event at hand and just breathe in the love and happiness of the surroundings. This breathing exercise allows my heart to be filled with renewed energy and love.

Traditionally, a wedding is intended to celebrate the union of two individuals who vow to love each other eternally, or at least until one of them drives the other crazy. But a wedding can also be a celebration for those in attendance—the opportunity to both renew and celebrate the love in one's own life. Whether it be the love for family, friends, or God, remembering the love that surrounds us all makes the wedding ceremony and festivities that much more meaningful and joyous.

After leaving the wedding that night, I wanted to capture these feelings of renewed love, so I grabbed my journal and headed to Huggo's Restaurant. Perched on the rocks at the ocean's edge in Kona

Village, Huggo's lovely and relaxing setting was a perfect place in which to gather my thoughts.

Filling page after page, my writing frenzy ended when I lifted my head to see a Hawaiian gentleman standing at my table. Shortly after introductions, Lance and I began having a wonderful conversation. We spoke for some time, focusing mostly on why he chooses to live on the Big Island.

"I was born here on the Big Island," he explained. "I've lived in other places and on other islands in Hawaii, but I always came back to the Big Island."

"Why this island?" I asked.

After several attempts to explain the draw of the Big Island, Lance quietly collected his thoughts and said, "My spirit lives here."

That said it all. To hear that Lance was so in touch with his spirit made it a no brainer for me to ask him for his answer to my question.

I enjoyed my time with Lance because his energy conveyed that he was quite content with the choices he had made in life. Lance was at peace knowing that he was exactly where he was supposed to be. How many of us can say that?

Lance

Life is living. Life is experience. Life is what you make of it.

Teachers on our Path

One night, I left my house and headed out for dinner. I didn't know where I was going, but I continued driving around. I had spent only a few minutes juggling options in my mind when I received words from Spirit.

Go to Bayside.

If you recall, Bayside Restaurant was the very restaurant where my book began. I didn't know the reason I was being sent there, but since I had already experienced so many wonderful moments from listening to Spirit, I knew not to question Him.

"OK, Bayside it is," I replied without hesitation or question.

I knew in my heart that something good was about to happen.

I ordered a glass of wine at the bar and started writing in my journal, waiting for the reason I was there to be revealed. Occasionally, I looked up from my journal to eye the bar, trying to spot a cute guy. Maybe, just maybe, Spirit brought me here to meet the man of my dreams. Unfortunately, that particular scenario didn't play out. However, I did notice that the man sitting on my right was watching me write in my journal. He later introduced himself as Dan.

"Are you writing a book?" he asked.

Well, that's probably just a good guess, I thought.

"Actually, I am," I answered. "Would you like to be in it?"

Whoa! Where did that come from? To say that I was surprised at myself for volunteering this information at the onset is an understatement. The truth is, my plan was not to tell a person about my book until we at least had spent a fair bit of time enjoying a meaningful conversation. Then, if a connection of some sort had developed, I'd ask them to be in my book. But for some unknown reason, I sensed that this moment with Dan was different. Somehow, it just felt right to ask him.

Dan listened intently to my explanation of what he would have to do to be in my book.

"Well, first tell me the question," he said.

"No," I drawled with a mischievous smile. "This is an all-or-nothing-at-all proposition. You have to agree to do it first. Then you get to know the question."

He shook his head. "Nah, that's OK," he said and abruptly turned away.

Conversation over.

Only a few seconds had passed when he spun back around.

"OK, ya got me," he said reluctantly. "I'll do it. What's the question?"

I handed Dan the paper that contained the question. He read it and then chuckled under his breath.

"I've been thinking about this very thing for the past year or so."

"What do you mean?" I asked.

Solemnly, Dan began to explain.

"Within the past eighteen months, my son was killed in a car accident. And my father died of a heart attack. And my brother died of liver failure." He looked up to catch my reaction.

No poker face here. I couldn't hide my doe-in-the-headlights expression.

With a quiet breath, Dan took hold of the pen and guided it in an effortless dance across the paper.

For several minutes I sat very still and watched Dan from the corner of my eye. I studied his face, wondering if I could get a sense of what he was feeling. I expected to see a dark cloud of sadness looming over his head. But there was no cloud. I thought that I might be able to see traces of bitterness or anger on his face. But there was none. Instead, I felt only a sense of peace around him, which baffled me. I mean really, how could anyone who had suffered such loss in such a short period of time feel peaceful? It was inconceivable. My only guess was that he must possess a very deep level of spirituality. Boy, was I right.

Dan

> Life is the preparation for the next level. We are put here for a reason, are placed in people's lives for a reason, and leave this plane for a reason. Our job is to live according to the laws of nature and God and inspire others to believe in the power of God.

After reading Dan's answer, I felt compelled to probe a bit further. Hesitantly, I asked a final question. "How have you survived?"

With eyes locked on mine, he quietly stated, "I believe in God."

The conversation was over. No more needed to be said.

With unfocused eyes, I stared into my half-empty glass of wine and tried to collect my thoughts about all the amazing things that happened in that one night: Spirit telling me to go to Bayside. Dan asking whether I was writing a book. Dan declining, and then quickly changing his mind. Then hearing his unbelievable story.

The only way it made any sense was to believe that there was a reason Spirit had directed me to that particular restaurant, on that particular night. It also made sense why I so quickly asked Dan to be in my book. Simply put: I was supposed to meet Dan.

All the more evidence for me to do what I'm told by Spirit.

◆   ◆   ◆

Holly and I began our relationship as cubicle neighbors in corporate America back in the '80s. From the start, we could see the contrast in our personalities. Holly was a free spirit who seemed to waltz effortlessly through life, whereas I was a serious, uptight workaholic struggling to advance my career. (Who says I had issues?) Even though our approaches to life were very different, we never judged the other. We simply accepted each other's choices.

As I look back, I think Holly probably got a good chuckle watching me stress out as I tried to make my mark. Her levity, however, would not have been at my expense. Instead, it would have come from a place of awareness and compassion; Holly (unlike me) could see that I was putting myself through something that was not good for my spirit. She did her best to help me find balance.

One day, after overhearing one of my rather tense telephone conversations, Holly decided to help lighten my mood. While sitting at my desk, deep in the throes of this conversation, tiny bubbles suddenly started floating over my cubicle wall. Yes, Holly had taken time away from her work to blow bubbles into my cubicle. This gave me the biggest laugh, and to say the least, the rest of my telephone conversation went much better!

Today, Holly still blows bubbles at me when she sees that I need them. Only now, the bubbles she sends my way are actually words of guidance, blessings, and love.

By the time you read this, I will have changed my write-up on Holly many times because she is a soul that I cannot easily capture in words. I struggle in my search for the perfect words and phrases to effectively describe the impact her love and wise teachings have had on me. Holly's commitment to personal growth, her courage to dig deep into herself for answers, and her capacity to give love, compassion, and acceptance are just a few qualities that are as much a part of Holly's being as the very air she breathes.

Words have also failed me when I have attempted to tell Holly what she means to me. In order for us to be released from the struggle over words, we have made a silent pact to honor what is said through our shared hugs, tears, and laughter.

I can only thank God for bringing Holly into my life, for she has shown me a better path.

Holly

> Meaning is what we as individuals make up about life. "Free will"
> is given to us to decide how we interpret life. As in this moment,
> I am giving meaning to my life in the form of communication
> with authenticity. I am feeling love and compassion toward
> friendship and being a friend. It is a gift. Life is a gift. Love is a
> gift. I choose to embrace this now in this moment.

Eileen is Holly's mom. She lived with me for a few months while she
danced her way through a transitional period of her life. It was a real
trip getting to know Holly's tango-dancing mom. I always found
myself comparing her mannerisms, philosophies, and personality
traits to Holly's. When I think of Eileen, I recall the old saying "the
fruit does not fall far from the tree," because I clearly see where the
seeds of Holly's love and spirit were born.

The best way to describe Eileen is to tell you that her smile starts at
her mouth and travels up and out through her eyes, bathing you with
love and acceptance with her soft gaze. I will also go so far as to say
that you can all but physically feel Eileen hugging you with her smiling eyes. As I see it, everything about Eileen's nature is a product of
her deeply rooted ability and desire to share her love, compassion, and
zest for life with those around her. From our short time together, I
can only hope that Eileen's joyful spirit continues to be contagious ...
and incurable.

I have learned a lot about life from this dynamic mother-daughter
duo and look forward to spending much more time in the warmth of
their love.

Eileen

> The meaning of life is whatever I make it to mean. It really
> doesn't mean anything unless I make it mean something. I can
> make it heaven or hell. Most of the time I've chosen Heaven. It's
> all about love when you come right down to it. Love really is the
> meaning of life.

And to make sure that Holly's husband, Scot, has his say ...

Scot

> Life is what happens whether you want it to or not. We all are at the controls when it comes to deciding which path we will lead life down, all the while hoping to find happiness and fulfillment.

Free Spirits All Around

I grew up in a very small town just south of New Orleans, Louisiana. (Yes, there is dry land south of New Orleans!) Outside of taking two family vacations, the geographic borders of my life extended no farther than a twenty-mile radius of my hometown. To say that my experience of the world was limited would be an understatement. As a kid, I may have had big dreams of seeing the world or doing great things in life, but if I did I don't remember sharing them with anyone. I probably was afraid of being incessantly ridiculed, especially if those dreams never came true. Or maybe I knew early on that I lacked the courage to even reach for my dreams.

Courage is a quality that I very much value because for the longest time, I could barely find an ounce of it in myself. Fear? Yes. I had tons of that. But courage? I had none. For most of my life (oh, let's say the first thirty years), I lacked the courage to rise up against the fear that was ever present in my being. I'm not saying that I spent my whole life sitting in a corner trembling with fear. But whenever it came time for me to test my mettle, fear took over and became as much a part of me as the blood running through my veins.

Instead of taking risks, I played it safe. Instead of believing in myself, I listened to and believed the criticisms of others. Of course, following this behavior pattern prevented me from living up to my full potential. It also lulled me into settling for a life that was merely *adequate*. Analyzing how and why I followed this course of behavior is either the subject for another book or maybe the makings for a good debate on nature vs. nurture. Whatever the reason, any dreams I had for my life stayed dormant for a long time.

In spite of my fear, or maybe because of it, I was always drawn to free spirits throughout my life. Those people who marched unafraid to the beat of a different drummer fascinated me because I was quite the opposite. While I played it safe, these free spirits possessed the courage to travel out of their comfort zone and set a course for the unknown.

Fortunately, many free spirits have influenced my life and helped me find the confidence to lay the groundwork for my own path, a path that would eventually lead me out of my comfort zone and into parts of myself yet to be discovered. And once I left "comfort-zone city," there was no turning back.

These days, I find that I am still drawn to free spirits. It was on a trip to Mendocino, California, December 2002, where I crossed paths with such a person. Her name was Marcelle. We met at Dick's Place, a local hangout in the center of town.

When I first looked at Marcelle with her long brown hair and youthful face, she seemed familiar to me, even though I knew we had never met. This feeling of familiarity persisted, and I stared at her for several minutes. Evidently she didn't think I was a weirdo for looking at her strangely, as conversation quickly ignited between us.

Twentysomething Marcelle entertained me with stories of the many places she had lived and traveled. As she chronicled her travels, I played the role of mental traveler and tried to imagine myself in all the same places. Hawaii, Alaska, New Mexico, Bolivia, and Paraguay are just a few of the places I can recall from her many stories.

After leaving Marcelle that night, I walked back to my hotel with many thoughts whirring through my head. I wondered what my younger days would have been like had I possessed more courage and less fear. And I thought about who I would be today had I followed a different path in life. I asked myself: Am I now on the right path? And where will my path lead in the future? More questions surfaced with each second.

Suddenly, I stopped walking and burst out laughing at my need to over analyze things. (Really … I could analyze lint if need be.) As I laughed at myself, I remembered Marcelle's last words to me: "when I get too serious about life, I allow my close friends to remind me to smile and to remember the humor."

How appropriate.

I continued my walk home with a calmed mind, a smile on my face, and Marcelle's words in my heart.

Marcelle

> As simply as I can put it, remember to celebrate the mystery every day. Remember humor. And always distinguish love and fear.

Musical Souls

I met my friend Steve about twenty years ago because our mutual friend Holly thought we should know each other. Holly knew us both quite well, and she was convinced that we would make an instant connection. She was right.

Steve is a working musician, and over the years, I have shown my support by becoming one of his loyal groupies. I mean really, how cool is it for a nerd like me to hang out with the band at a gig or to be let into a club by telling the doorman, "I'm with the band"!

In the early days of our relationship, Steve's presence in my life was more like that of a thread weaving in and out through a piece of fabric. Marriages, divorces, and relocations made our contact sporadic at best. However, over time, Steve became an integral part of my life. Today, he is more like a continuous thread of golden yarn that is tightly woven into the fabric of my life, adding both depth and complexity to its design.

Steve and I share a common philosophy: always be open to learning. We are especially open to learning from each other. At times, we tend to get so wrapped up in our search for knowledge that we don't even notice when we transition from the role of student to that of teacher. In fact, we are both a bit reluctant to wear the label of teacher. Speaking for myself, I can be comfortable wearing that label only by frequently and audibly acknowledging the fact that "I teach/ preach what I most need to learn."

When I look at Steve, I see the type of person I want to be when I grow up. He is not judgmental; I have yet to hear Steve speak ill of anyone (except maybe a politician or two). Even when he has seen me at my worst, he has never judged me. He lives steadfastly by his philosophy to love and accept people for who they are. I love that about him.

My yoga pillow sums up Steve the best. On it is an embroidered quote from Oprah: surround yourself with only people who are going to lift you higher. Well, this describes Steve perfectly. When I'm down, he has the ability to comfort me for as long as it takes my spirit to mend and then lift me high enough so that I can again see the Light on my own.

I am not sure whether Steve was blessed with all of these gifts at birth or learned it all from great teachers along his path. All I know is that whenever I have a broken heart or spirit, the safest place for me to surrender and heal is wrapped in Steve's loving energy. I absolutely adore him and remain in awe of his ability to love. I will forever be grateful that he chooses to share his love with me.

There is no doubt in my mind that when Steve reaches the pearly gates, his reward for living a good life will be an invitation to jam with the band. I just hope he remembers to tell the doorman to let me in.

Steve

> To serve, learn, love, and experience as much as possible. Find out the one thing that gives you the most pleasure and satisfaction and DO IT! The blessing of life gives us the opportunity to create whatever reality we want as long as we surrender ourselves with the right people. Keeping this idea in our hearts and minds will take us a long way. If I live each day to the fullest, not taking anything for granted, and I am 100 percent honest with myself, I will always do the right thing and will enjoy a rich and bountiful life.

I met Bruce through Steve several years ago at one of their gigs. (Bruce has forgiven me for not remembering our first meeting.) I must admit that the first time I remember meeting Bruce I thought he was going to end up being nothing more than a jokester because he was forever teasing me about my relationship with Steve. You see Bruce could not understand how Steve and I could have such a close relationship yet be only platonic friends. But the more Bruce and I crossed paths and the more time we spent talking, the more our conversations plunged into some rather deep subjects. Fortunately, what surfaced from these conversations was Bruce's deeper side.

I am nowhere close to being able to say that I "know" Bruce, but I have already experienced the duality of his personality—light and breezy on one side with a flip side of intellectual and emotional depth. I enjoy his complexity and love that he allowed both sides to come through in his answer to my meaning of life question.

If I had to sum up what I have learned from Bruce, it would be that I need to lighten up sometimes and to continue smiling from the heart.

Bruce

> I can be deep on the topic or simple. I'll try simple for now. "The meaning of life is" …

1. Be born.

2. Get a good education and take advantage of all that is available to you in that educational field.

3. Find a good-paying job and advance.

4. Find the right person, marry, and have a family (the number of children is optional, but we do have overpopulation, so keep it low; 1–3 kids at the most.)

5. Be responsible for yourself. Nothing is worse than being dependant on others or institutions to see you through life's troubles. A little TLC is OK, but don't abuse it!

6. Grow old, retire, and have fun—travel.

7. Stay healthy and die of natural causes (hopefully in your sleep).

Deep meaning of life …

Enjoy all that is laid in front of you. There will be good and bad times, but if you cannot enjoy all that is around you—the sky, the mountains, the desert, the sea, the wind, hot, cold, people, etc.—then there is no meaning.

Choose your path, inspirational or not, but be honest with yourself in your beliefs and try not to compromise in those beliefs just to fit in. Try to be unique no matter how hard. Contribute every day no matter how big or small.

It's all good! Have a nice day.

My Love Life Is a Zit

I stay true to a very old-fashioned rule when it comes to dating a friend's ex, whether it is an ex-boyfriend or an ex-husband. Simply put, I won't do it because I put a high value on my friendships. To me, dating someone's ex would be disrespectful to the friendship. Having said that, I do know that exceptions to the rule can be tempting.

In this case, Steve was the ex of an ex-friend of mine. Since the friend was no longer in my life, one would think that the no-dating-an-ex rule would no longer apply. Technically, I would agree. I would be lying if I said that I wasn't flattered by his attention toward me. However, every time I looked at Steve, images of him sucking face with my friend flashed before my eyes. There was just no way that I could date him with this picture in my mind, so I turned down his advances.

I have never told Momma this story for the simple reason that she already thinks that I'm weird for remaining single for well over a decade after my divorce. If I would have told her that I actually turned away an interested fella, she might have had me committed. You see, Momma still wants me to have a man in my life so that I have someone to "take care" of me. (Talk about being old-fashioned.) She means well. In her day, it was rare for a woman to have the means (financial or emotional) to live a happy and successful life independent of a man. Being without a partner was just unheard of. But times change.

Today, many single people have had to learn to walk through life independently because the dry spells of dating often get longer as the years go by. My perspective on not having a steady love life can best be compared to how I deal with having a zit.

Picture yourself in this scenario. You are on your way out the door for a night on the town. You take one last look in the mirror. Your hair is looking unbelievably good. You are looking hot in your "skinny" jeans. And your makeup? Flawless, if you do say so yourself. But there, lurking on your chin, is a red bump. You know very well what it is, and you also know what it is going to turn into.

In that moment, you decide your fate: Am I going to let this zit affect my life? Do I get upset, depressed, or neurotic over it? Should I cancel my plans and spend the night comforted by a tub of rocky road? Do I lock myself in the house until it goes away?

Much like the zit on my face, not having a love life can be annoying, painful, and an overall unpleasant situation. It's very easy to look into the mirror at my life and only focus on the fact that I am alone, meaning only that I am without a partner. In fact, there have been times in my past when this was all I thought about. And believe me, there have also been plenty of nights when a bowl (or three) of rocky road has eased my pain.

Fortunately, I have learned to put this zitty aspect of my life into perspective. Now when I walk in front of a mirror, I stand far enough away so that I can see my entire reflection. I stand there until I see a balanced view of myself—all the good things and all the bad—and then I say out loud: "this too shall pass."

Steve

> I thought I had met the woman of my dreams. I was smitten by her smile, her look; what a woman. Men and women search the world for the above. They never attain the meaning. The meaning of life is to participate.

The "Tired of Dating" Club

I will never date again!

Over and over again, I hear single men and women say that when a certain age is reached one either becomes disillusioned by the dating game or abandons the game altogether. Perhaps it happens when you reach a point in life when it just takes too much energy to open your heart and trust someone again. Surely, we can all count the hundreds of times that we have risked opening our hearts only to have some numbskull walk in and rip it to shreds! (Bitter, table for one?)

So it isn't far-fetched to say that most single people have thought about giving up on the dating world at least once in their lives. I know I've heard myself say, "Tonight, I will neither pluck my eyebrows nor shave my legs nor wear that sexy lingerie that pricks at my skin all night. And forget about wearing that special come-fall-in-love-with-me perfume." And you dare ask why I'm still single?

When we're deep in the throes of our own personal dating hell, I think it's human nature to believe that we are the only one on Earth experiencing such bad luck. *Everyone in the entire world is in love tonight … except me!* Of course, since we're also rational human beings, we know this is simply not the case. Even still, our minds still go there.

It's especially during these frustrating times that misery loves company. Not that we revel in the fact that there is another miserable soul walking around (well, maybe sometimes), but it sure does help to hear that unmistakable sigh of dating exasperation coming from someone else besides the person in the mirror.

With dinner fork in hand and my nose buried in my journal, I still noticed Robert sitting next to me. A quick glance was all that was needed to see the sadness in his face. I wasn't sure why, but my heart went out to him—maybe because I recognized his expression as one I have occasionally spotted in my mirror.

Robert's face, although handsome, sagged as though it had melted over time. My initial guess was that this wasn't solely due to the aging process but instead caused by the weight of emotional residue left behind from years of trying to find that special someone. I really wanted to be wrong about this. Unfortunately, with only a few minutes of conversation, Robert validated my guess.

I learned that although Robert didn't currently have that "special someone" in his life, he did indeed have a life filled with special love. Robert possessed what I consider to be the most special love of all: the love of a child.

After answering my question, he shared a bit of the story behind it.

He told me that the three orphans he referred to in his answer are the children he and his wife, Virginia, adopted from Korea. The couple adopted the children after they had lost two natural-born children—one at birth, the other at age seven. In 1984, cancer took Virginia, leaving Robert alone to raise his three children.

As I say over and over, I do not believe in accidents. I think there was a higher reason that motivated me to begin a conversation with Robert. Maybe that moment gave me the opportunity to help comfort the lonely soul of another because I do believe that when a person shares his or her loneliness with another, both souls are lifted. I also believe that if everyone chose to believe that we are brothers and sisters on this Earth, then maybe there would always be someone sitting at our side, ready to listen to our story of how life has left us feeling a bit tired.

I ask you to never underestimate the power of giving your smile to a stranger or lending an ear to listen to their heart. These simple acts can heal more pain than you can imagine—theirs and your own.

Robert

> Life is to leave the world better than which you arrived. Life is providing the means for the unfortunate to thrive and prosper. In my case, this is taking three orphans from a third-world country and giving them a chance in life.

Conrad was one of the gentlemen I met during my (short-lived) adventure in the world of online dating. Although there was no love connection between us, I still enjoyed our date.

I giggle at myself every time I think about having gone online looking for Mr. Right. Even though I've heard success stories of people marrying after meeting online, I had scoffed at the idea of online dating for so very long.

You see I tend to be very old-fashioned, believing in the more traditional ways of dating. I also admit to at times refusing to adjust my behavior to be more in line with modern shifts in societal attitudes or behaviors regarding dating (for example, the notion of a woman making the first move or being the first one to call). It is for these reasons, along with the fact that I'm very selective, that I choose not to date—well, unless there is real potential for something meaningful.

My reluctance toward casual dating goes back to when I was first allowed to date (if I can remember that far back!). During my younger days, I never accepted just any old date, nor did I date someone just because I couldn't stand being alone. Even the pressure of "date night" didn't break me. And so far, I have yet to date a man for a free meal. I prefer not to create that kind of karma in my life.

Because of my choices, some people have labeled me as being too independent or too picky. OK, I can own up to that. But the one thing that I have learned in life is that all of my choices come at a price. For me, the price of staying true to myself, as well as respecting others along the way, will be willingly paid in full every time.

Conrad

> I see life as a gift and a conscious choice. We can choose anything we like. I believe before we are born, we choose to come to Earth (in this case) to learn lessons we can only attain here, that is, if we want to learn humility, we may choose to be born to a family in Bangladesh, and loose legs and become a street beggar. If then, at the end of our life when we reunite with our spiritual self in the light, we get to analyze, not judge if we have accomplished our mission of learning to be humble. We all have missions, and I believe if we truly follow our hearts, we can accomplish our spiritual path to become more perfect spiritual beings from the environment of Earth situations.
>
> It is the seemingly challenging times that allow us to stretch; the people who push our buttons that are the gifts in life. We are the architects of our destiny. Life doesn't just happen. We can be and get anything we choose; just ask. I believe it is also important to then recognize other people's life choices without judgment, and honor and support them to be who they want to be or the illusion they think they are.
>
> … And to always recognize the God in every living thing and person. Seeing and spreading that light.

As you may have noticed, I often write in my journal while out in public. Of course, some people may accuse me of writing in public as a way of drawing attention to myself … Do you really think I would 'fess up to that? But when it attracts the attention of really nice guys, I choose to live out the adventure. In my case, these adventures most always garnered material for my book.

Rocky

> The meaning of life, in simple terms … it's my children and the joy that they have given me over the years. What they have taught

me now makes me a better man and I know that I'm ready to share that with a significant other. Life is too short, and we don't tell people that we love them enough. So in my humble opinion, the meaning of life is learning to love. Hopefully in our life, we will have someone to love more than life itself.

Farhad

To make a difference in this world in some way. To me, life is a process and not a destination. In the process, one must hope to keep on learning, giving, and moving forward. One must be brave enough to stand for the right cause, not give up, and do his/her best to stand for the right thing and leave this world with a mark. That mark should be a positive contribution to mankind/humanity/world. In other words, the meaning of life is a life with meaning. Moving in that direction is never too late. And once someone moves in that direction, the joy, happiness, etc. of this enlightenment is so high that he/she will experience heaven!

Celebrate being alive!

More times than not, when a guy and his buddy spot me writing, I inevitably receive an opening line such as "Are you writing down everything we say?" Understanding that most men are plagued with fear of rejection, I do applaud and graciously acknowledge most any attempt a man makes to start a conversation. The fact is, there are a lot of great guys out there, but they are far too shy for their own good. So when Shawn used this same opening line, I took the bait and played along.

After a rather flirtatious conversation, Shawn asked for my number. Even though I was a bit surprised that I gave it to him (a rarity for me), I was not at all surprised when he didn't call after several weeks passed.

Why was I not surprised? Oh, gee, maybe it was because he hadn't even bothered to write down my number. Yet to soften the blow of not receiving a call, I did what most sophisticated and highly intelligent women do … I concocted a story to appease my ego.

I told myself, *Of course he's interested in me. The only reason he hasn't called is because he's probably just a bit embarrassed that he forgot my number.*

Sure, the story lacked creativity, but facing the reality that he just wasn't interested in me seemed far worse. The end result? I thought I would try once again to be a "modern woman," and I called him. (Desperate, party of one?)

I told myself that I would call Shawn just for fun. I then decided to enhance the entertainment value of the conversation by not immediately telling him who I was. *Let's see whether he can guess who I am.* Instead of identifying myself, I chose to merely drop a few *obvious* hints as to how and where we met.

To cut to the chase, let me just say that Shawn listened to all of the hints and then offered his best guesses as to my identity. "Are you Jennifer? Susan? Tracy?" he asked.

Well, you get the picture. After a few minutes of rather "enlightened" conversation (sarcasm intended), I politely thanked him for his time and quickly ended the conversation. End of story.

Once again, I was reminded that there are far too many of these guys out there. We all know the type … guys who still get a kick out of getting as many phone numbers as they can by the end of a night, never intending to call any of them. And, yes, according to my male friends, women are equally guilty.

In this particular case, I already knew that I was responsible for creating my own headache. To alleviate the pain, I chose to take the best medicine I knew: a large dose of humor followed by several minutes of chanting "Rejection is God's protection."

Shawn

Experience. Fun. Laughter. Friends. Sorrow. Sadness. Freedom. Security. Marriage. Divorce. Accomplishment. Pride. Honesty. Integrity.

How Would Daddy Answer?

You must know from the start that Daddy passed away in 1995. However, from the moment I started writing this book, I knew that I wanted Daddy's answer to be a part of it. After all, who better to know the answer to the meaning of life than someone from the other side? So for my book's sake, and for some other personal reasons, I have done my best to "channel" Daddy's answer.

No, I am not a medium of any sort, although I do have great respect for people with such abilities. I readily admit that I have taken creative license to publish what I received as Daddy's answer.

For the longest time, I had put off talking to Daddy about sending me his answer. I wanted to make sure that I was in the right place—emotionally and physically—when I spoke to him.

I don't mind sharing that whenever I decide to talk to Daddy, I consciously choose the time and place. I will also go so far as to control which thoughts of him I allow to nestle in my mind. On a good day, I can think of Daddy or even have a conversation with him and be able to remain centered, knowing that although he is in a better place, he is still with me in spirit. But boy, oh boy! It is those *other* days that really knock me for a loop … the times when even a fleeting thought of him will spark emotions in me so strong and raw that I am brought back to feeling the way I did on the day of his passing.

Even though I talk with Daddy frequently, I am amazed that I can still be caught off guard by the recurring pain and inevitable deluge of tears. Now, I do believe that a good cry cleanses the soul, but having such a cry in the middle of a grocery store is never a good idea! So, picking the time and place helps me keep unexpected emotional displays a private affair. Therefore, before I "channeled" Daddy's answer, I made sure that the time, place, and my emotional strength were just right.

My story of Daddy's passing is one of the best stories of my life. I know that sounds strange, but I love this story because it tells of two people in a shaky relationship who come together in the nick of time.

I confess that I had always wanted a relationship with Daddy like the Beave had with his dad, Ward. You know how it went ... Ward would sit the Beave down and have warm, loving talks with him, even when the Beave did something goofy. There was no yelling. No silent treatment. No toe-curling tension. Sure, Ward's patience was tested from time to time by the Beave's antics, but Ward always displayed a calm, understanding demeanor. At the end of their talks, the Beave would be sent off with a hug and a smile.

Of course I knew that wanting this was a fantasy, but when things in my home life got a bit testy, I chose to escape to fantasyland to wait out the storm. I was like the Beave (in terms of the antics), but Daddy was quite the opposite of Ward.

I could be generous and describe Daddy as the "strong, silent" type, with an emphasis on *silent*—that is, until he exploded in anger. Or I could peel back the veneer of that description and label him the more modern (psychobabble) translation of *emotionally unavailable*. Either way, the distance between us was palpable.

Even though we lived under the same roof, Daddy was a stranger to me for most of my life. I feared him. I obeyed him. I loved him. But I never knew him or his past. Daddy was not someone who ever volunteered such information. And if you are wondering if I ever asked him questions about his past, I learned at a very early age not to go there unless I wanted to be answered with silence, or worse. Being around Daddy was like walking through a minefield. You never knew when your step would trigger an explosion.

Daddy was quite a moody person, to say the least. Early on, I learned to start my day by first checking to see what kind of mood he was in before opening my mouth. His bad moods were intense, anger-filled, and so frequent, that I eventually mastered a coping technique for dealing with them. I disappeared—emotionally and physically. Unfortunately, I was given ample opportunity to hone this skill. Disappearing physically was easy; I just stayed out of the house or hid in my room until the air cleared. But disappearing emotionally was a bit trickier and probably harder for someone else to understand.

I used to think of my disappearing act as my way of going into a Zen state of mind, not that I actually knew what that was when I was a child. But I had once heard it explained in an old movie as an emotionally neutralized state of mind that you place yourself in when faced with a dangerous situation. To reach this neutralized state, you release all negative energy—fear or anger—from your entire being so as not to antagonize the source of danger. After releasing your negative or threatening energy, what is left behind is equivalent to an empty shell. How much of my childhood was spent as a walking empty shell?

Now, whether it was a Zen thing or not doesn't matter. All I know is that the trick sure came in handy living in a house where talking back or even having the wrong expression on your face would land you in a heap of trouble.

That was pretty much how my relationship with Daddy played out until I was about sixteen and the only child left at home. All of the troublemakers—my siblings—had moved out of the house. I guess with less chaos in the house, Daddy and I were able to move around each other in a more peaceful way. When I turned eighteen, I moved out of the house to attend college, and a few years later, I moved to California.

As the years passed, Daddy's hard edges seemed to soften. The more he softened, the less I feared him. The less I feared him, the more I was able to drop my defenses and see him more clearly. It took some time, but I finally was able to see Daddy as a person who simply did the best he knew how to do. Once I could acknowledge him as a normal flawed human being, I was then able to forgive him ... for whatever it was that I thought he had done to me in my childhood. It was only through the power of forgiveness that I began to connect with Daddy.

In April 1995, my parents flew to California for a visit. When Daddy stepped off the plane, I saw for the first time an old man. The years had indeed taken a toll. Seeing Daddy in such an advanced, aged state had such an impact that it left me with one thought: *it is time to start preparing for his death.* It was a very powerful and disturbing thought, to say the least.

Upon arriving at my house, we settled in the living room. Within a matter of seconds, Daddy locked eyes with me.

"So, how long will it take you to get home if something happens?" he asked.

I knew exactly what he was asking. *How long after getting "the call" would it take to get to his deathbed?* I also knew why he was asking it. He, too, was preparing for his death.

Although I was shocked by his candor, I was thrilled to finally have him ask me a real question.

"Well, you just flew here," I said holding his gaze. "It'll take me the same amount of time."

I suddenly found that I had the strength to confront Daddy openly, honestly, and lovingly. It was a first for me.

Without taking my eyes off his, I continued. "But if I can't make it back home in time, you have to promise me something."

"OK." He was right there with me. He was open to hearing what I had to say and actually *wanted* to hear what I had to say.

"Well, let me offer a few options for you." I grabbed Spirit's hand and continued with strength and courage. "First, you must stay there until I arrive."

He nodded in agreement.

"Or, if you can't wait until I arrive, you have to at least stay in the room until I get there."

Again, he nodded without hesitation.

"But if you have to go, come and tell me that you're passing."

"OK," he agreed, solemnly and knowingly.

In that moment, the powerful energy of our connection embraced us for what seemed like an eternity. *Eternity, indeed.*

The air around us felt thin and fragile, so much so that I was afraid to even breathe. I feared that even the slightest noise or movement would break the magical spell that had been cast over our conversation. But as is my nature, I gently pushed the envelope a bit further. Still holding his gaze, I dared to test the strength of our newfound connection.

"If I can't make it back in time, let's do it … right here and now. Tell me what you would say to me if I was there." He knew what I was saying: *Let's have the deathbed conversation now.*

Without missing a beat, he said, "I want you to know that I love you. I always have. I know that I didn't tell you very often …" His words trailed off.

Nothing more needed to be said, for in that moment there was forgiveness—forgiveness for anything and everything that we may have done in the past to hurt each other. All the wounds were instantly healed. All the pain dissolved. Never before had I felt my heart more open and full of love than in that moment with Daddy.

Four months later, I went home to be with my family. Daddy had just been diagnosed with having an aneurysm of the aorta and was scheduled for immediate surgery. After the four-hour surgery, blood clots began to form and he was immediately brought back to surgery for an additional four hours. Daddy left the operating room in a coma.

Several hours passed while we waited at Daddy's bedside in ICU. At the end of the day, I whispered in Daddy's ear, telling him that I had to leave to catch my flight back to California. I told him that I would call him once he was out of ICU and back in his regular room.

My sisters drove me to the airport, both wearing the same expression of disbelief on their faces, as if silently asking me, *Have you lost your mind?* They lovingly asked whether I was sure I wanted to leave, and I assured them that it was the right thing to do because I was certain that Daddy was going to be OK. (Can you say "denial"?)

While on my way to the airport, unbeknownst to me, the doctor was telling my family that Daddy would not make it through the night.

As I approached my departure gate, I passed a group of pay phones. Nothing strange about that, but I couldn't stop staring at them. I stared at the phones from the moment I approached them until I was well past. Since my mind was already in such a haze, I didn't even try to understand why I was doing this. I merely shrugged it off and proceeded to the check-in desk to receive my boarding pass.

I turned away from the desk and heard the message in my head: *go call your momma.*

I immediately turned on my heels and headed for the pay phones—the same group of phones that I had just stared down.

I called ICU. My brother received the call.

"Did you hear your page?" he asked.

"No, what page?"

As soon as the words left my mouth, I heard a page over the loudspeaker. "Louise Lewis, please pick up the white courtesy phone."

In that moment, while standing at the pay phone, I could feel Daddy's presence with me. And then I knew. I knew that he had kept his promise to me. Of all the options I had given him, Daddy had chosen to "come to me and tell me that he was ready to pass."

As a result of my experience with Daddy's passing, I feel even more certain of the existence of "the other side." Knowing this allows me to walk through life with a greater sense of peace.

Daddy

> I continue to be so very proud of you and regret not telling you this more. I now understand how much you needed to hear this when you were growing up. I have learned so much since I am here. You know, kind of like the old V8 commercial when the guy slaps his forehead with his palm and says something like "I should've had a V8." Well, Lou, that's how it's been for me here. I've been shown all the things I should have done or said. And for that analytical mind of yours, I want you to know that the "would've, could've, should've" stuff is not done with judgment here.
>
> But I would say that the meaning of life is to live in your heart. Nowhere else. See with your heart. Listen with your heart. Pass your words through your heart before speaking them because your spirit, your life energy, lives here. And if you're not living with this flow running through your body, then you're merely existing. And that is such a waste of your time on Earth.
>
> I also love it when we talk. Remind the others to keep talking to me as well. I love you all.

The answer from my brother Zeke, follows Daddy's answer because Zeke is Daddy's only son. As such, they shared a strong and unique bond that neither my sisters nor I could ever match. Therefore, I thought it only fitting that Zeke and Daddy stayed close in print as well.

It has taken a long time for me to address my thoughts about my brother. For the longest time (about the first thirty years of my life), we didn't have a close relationship at all. "Estranged" would be a more accurate description of our relationship.

Zeke had always been a pain-in-the-butt brother, and right or wrong, I was convinced that his sole purpose in life was to torment me. Back then, I never spent time analyzing or worrying about our relationship or lack thereof. That obsession came later. Instead, I just figured that his behavior toward me was either typical of brothers or that he simply didn't like me. Unfortunately, he convinced me of the latter by always telling me that my sister Diane was his favorite. What a butthead! But if truth were known, I was jealous and wanted him to like me, too. Admitting this, however, would have left me even more open to attack, and the last thing I needed was to provide him with more ammunition for future fights.

As the baby of the family—yes, the special child—I learned early on from both my parents and siblings that it wasn't safe to show my hurt feelings. Ever. I knew that it wasn't wise to ever admit to the pain caused when someone's slings and arrows had made a direct hit on my heart, no matter how bad a wound it made.

Instead, I did what I was taught. I hid my feelings behind protective walls of anger and took my own best shots in defense. You see, in my family, we used verbal firepower. Sarcasm and criticism were our weapons of choice to keep the enemy at bay. We fought fire with fire to the bitter end, and as a result, we all became masters in the art of verbal sparring. Blood was never shed, but boy did we get a lot of practice inflicting pain on one another. We were even better at hiding our pain

For the longest time, I never understood why we acted like that toward one another. Why was everyone being so mean? Why did we think it necessary to attack one another? The answers to these questions and more came to me much later in life. It was then that I truly realized the negative impact of my family environment on my ability to trust people or to be open and vulnerable in a relationship. Even though I was aware of the possibility that I was a product of my environment, I knew that I had to own up to the role I played in the chaos. I had to take responsibility for choosing to buy into that kind of behavior. (I think it was Dr. Phil who said something like "You choose the behavior, you choose the consequence.")

I desperately needed to confront the reasons for my behavior and address the choices that I had made with my family. To accomplish this, I first had to make another choice, a conscious choice to step onto a path of growth—both emotionally and spiritually. Eventually, this path of personal development allowed me to tap into a source of energy that gave me the strength to begin figuring out the answers to two questions: What the heck was up with my family? And what the heck was up with me?

It was during this time that I chose to confront Zeke with the truth of how I felt about our relationship. Very simply, I shared with him thoughts and feelings of the past that needed to be resolved in my heart. Without giving him a reason to duck for protection, I told him, "I do not know who you are. And I don't want to continue having a brother who is a stranger. And by the way, let's drop our weapons. Once and for all."

Fortunately, he agreed, and we both surrendered.

I will not bore you with the details of my relationship work with Zeke. But through our hard work, which included over a decade of extreme honesty and plenty of tears, we arrived at a loving place of healing and forgiveness. Even now, I cry as I share with you how very happy I am that my relationship with Zeke continues to develop on a much higher level than ever before. Unlike the tears of the past, today's tears are caused by an overflow of joy rather than hurt. When I compare how I felt about Zeke back then to how I feel now, my heart (and eyes) runneth over!

I am grateful that Zeke chose to walk with me along the path that led us back to each other. The journey has helped me to experience the meaning of the quote "The truth shall set you free."

I guess one day I will have to apologize for the "butthead" comment!

Zeke

I really don't know. For some reason, the Almighty chose to make us in His image. And why, I have no idea. And therefore, we are born, and I think we are supposed to live like he would want us to, as he wants ... as a Christian. And the definition of Christian is Christlike. As a Catholic, you are taught to believe in the Trinity, and Christ is one third of the Trinity ... his Son. And his Son and the Father gave of themselves to redeem us from our sins.

So, to be Christlike is to live our lives as Christ lived his. To be generous, kind, and helpful to others who are less fortunate. If

I am able to achieve that for any portion of my life, I will feel that I have meaning to my life. Without accomplishing this task, for even a very short time, life would have little meaning.

To Be Blessed With Sisters

My two sisters, Diane and Tina, mean the world to me. They are my best friends. Many times over the years, I have thought about what my life would be like if they were to leave this world before me. If that day should happen, well then, darlin', you can just put me in the casket with them. To be faced with the possibility of going through life without a sister is unimaginable.

The very thought of Diane and Tina not in my (physical) life scares me to death (no pun intended)—so much so that I actually once tried to duplicate the kind of relationship that I have with my sisters with that of one of my girlfriends. I hoped that one day that special sister bond would magically develop between us. My thinking, albeit idiotic, was that if I could "clone" the relationship I had with my sisters, I would not hurt so much when they died. Needless to say, my friend and I had little success in forming the same kind of bond. Not only was it impossible to re-create a sister's bond, but it was also far too great an expectation to put upon another relationship.

Thankfully, I have come to accept the fact that it is futile to try to replace my sisters; the bond between us is very special and cannot be duplicated.

Now, instead of dreading the day when my sisters are no longer with me, I allow Spirit to transform my fear into a greater appreciation of their presence in my life—in the here and now.

I have been truly blessed with the gift of sharing life with two sisters. Of course, you never would have caught me saying that when I was a kid. I mean no disrespect, but I feel badly for women who don't have sisters like mine. I have not yet found the words to describe the love I have for my gorgeous, loving sisters.

I will tell you about Diane first.

Diane is older than I am by two years. As kids, we bickered constantly, and if Diane ever had the opportunity to speak to you, the first story out of her mouth would be the one about the time I tried to kill her in the bathtub. Well, that is her version of the story and she loves telling it. To this day, she tries to get sympathy from anyone who will listen. My side of the story is that I merely gave her a light tap on the shoulder. Was it my fault that she accidentally slipped and fell into the bathtub? Of course there were no witnesses to the incident, so it remains her word against mine. Since this is my book, guess whose version wins out?

If you were to ask me what I enjoy most in life, I would have to say it would be making Diane laugh. She has one of those cute, infectious laughs. (Unfortunately, I am the snorter of the family!) Diane and I have the most fun when we come down with such a serious case of the giggles that one of us is crying through the laughter while the other is trying not to pee in her panties.

Diane means so very much to me because she plays so many roles in my life—that of sister, best friend, confidante, patient (with me as therapist), and therapist (with me as patient). But most of all, I see Diane as a role model for how to keep alive the spunk of a true southern lady.

My love for Diane is so deep and profound that I thank God every day for blessing my life with her presence. I am also very thankful that Diane and I have grown into well-adjusted people, with our days of squabbling far away in the past. However, just in case we do have a falling out in the future, we have agreed to stay away from bathtubs.

Diane

> Learn from the experienced. Share with the less fortunate. Give to those you care for. And above all, embrace life to the fullest every day!

There is a five-year age difference between Tina and me. Five years doesn't sound like much of a time span now, but when I was young the age difference seemed immense. As kids, Tina and I were never close; our level of interaction was low to nonexistent. It was not, however, just the age difference that kept us apart; we also had nothing in common. In fact, we were so different that I'm sure there were times when we both wondered if the other was adopted. We later agreed that it was Diane who was the adopted one.

It sounds strange to say, but I know very little about Tina during our early years. My first memories of Tina were in being told that she was the "brainy" one in the family. Throughout her school days, Tina made straight As. She was very focused on her studies and later became a nurse. In contrast, my grades were fair at best, and I chose instead to major in the social aspects of school until I decided what I wanted to do with my life. (For the record, I am still trying to decide what I want to be when I grow up.)

For about the first two decades of my life, Tina and I merely operated on the periphery of each other's world, never really getting involved with the other. I write this with no judgment. We were both busy just trying to survive our own day-to-day lives.

I married during my early twenties, and it was only then did Tina and I share a common life experience. As married ladies, we had stuff to talk about. But it really wasn't until after my divorce several years later that my relationship with Tina began to grow. If there were anything good that came out of my divorce, it would be that it fueled my desire to begin examining the many not-so-wise choices that I had made in life, especially when it came to relationships.

Knowing that I had to take responsibility for my part in what went wrong in my relationships, I began a self-help crusade of sorts, trying to find the answer to the question: why am I like this in relationships? In reading through mountains of self-help books, I began to reprogram my mind, body, and soul (what I call the Trilogy of Being) with information and tools to use that would help me address conflict with love rather than anger. Armed with this knowledge, I began to untangle the relationships in my life by coming clean with my family members, especially my siblings.

In so many words, I confessed to each of them: "I really don't know who you are as a person, and I would like to have a real relationship with you. Are you game?" Thank God they all agreed.

These days, Tina and I enjoy a close relationship that was made possible by a pact we made long ago. We agreed to work through our issues from the past and to forgive and learn from our mistakes as we moved forward. It worked wonders. No longer are there any lingering feelings of separation between us; the distance has all melted away.

I have come to rely on Tina's spirit, grace, and internal strength that come shining through even in the most difficult of times. For when I am in need, she is one of the first people to lend an ear and to offer comfort and support.

As for the differences that remain between us, I have come to understand that I learn so much from Tina *because* she is so different from me. Come to think of it, I would bet the farm that Tina has no idea how much I have learned from her over the years. I must tell her soon....

Tina

Life Is a Test

Of courage …
  To wake up each day and face what life has to offer—the challenges, trials and tribulations, beauty and splendor, joys and sorrows, and accomplishments.

Of faith …
  To believe in a Supreme Being who created all we know and experience. To believe in good and evil and that anything is possible.

Of love …
  To love unconditionally with a pure heart and to forgive with a pure heart and to forgive when we have been wronged.

And Then There's Momma

Momma has witnessed a lot of change in me over the years. Along the way, there were times when she freaked out over some of the changes I made because she was unable to understand or agree with them. Some of my choices in life have challenged her view of how the world should be, or more accurately, challenged her view on how she wanted *my* world to be. But even though she questioned most every choice I made, all in all, I think she would now agree that every change has improved my life by advancing my personal growth. Thankfully, the growth I experienced led me to a higher path of learning, a path on which I invited her to join. Unfortunately, it was Daddy's passing that forced Momma onto a growth path of her own.

When Daddy passed away, Momma was left alone for the first time in her life. As a young girl, she had gone from her father's house straight to her husband's house. Being alone proved to be difficult for her, but consequently, it was during this time that I found Momma to be the most open and vulnerable that I had ever experienced in my life.

Momma and I always got along, and for the most part, we had a fairly open line of communication. However, it wasn't until after Daddy's passing that we began to actually have deep, meaningful conversations about getting along with and without people in our life, love, sorrow, regrets—pretty much all topics that fall under *the meaning of life*. (What a great lead-in to my book!)

To be quite honest, Momma always had a place in my book because, well, she's my Momma (and Catholic guilt would have prevented me from not asking her). But since I had been able to get to know Momma on a much deeper level, outside of the confines of the mother-daughter roles, I was so excited to have her be a part of my adventure.

I asked Momma to be in my book during her visit at Christmas. I think she was shocked to hear that I was writing a book, but due to the nature of our conversations over the past few years, I don't think she was at all surprised with the subject matter I chose. Without hesitation, she agreed to be in my book and immediately began writing her answer.

Momma

> My meaning of life is to always be close to people and to be caring and loving to everyone I meet. Life is so rewarding to have God in my life. To start each day with His wisdom so I can share it with others.

Let me stop you here. Anyone who knows Momma would say, "You mean this is all she wrote?" You see, Momma does like to talk. A lot. Therefore, I was a bit surprised at the brevity of her answer but accepted it with much appreciation. However, I was not altogether surprised when a week later, I received a letter from her that included an addendum to her original answer. May I suggest you pour yourself a glass of wine, put up your feet, and read the rest of Momma's answer. It may take a while.

> … The more I thought, the more I realized that my answer to your question was OK, but not really what life means. To me, what it really means is to be able to express to others all the blessings God has bestowed on me. First and foremost, that He has me as His child; that my parents instilled in me the importance of having God always first in my life. And secondly, the four beautiful children He has loaned to me to teach. I am so proud of the

four of you because you are all very loving, caring, thoughtful, and sharing. That is so important to a parent, and He has helped me to succeed at that. For one to be able to do the same and to share with others the wisdom to help people that need help with different things. To help when they are hurting, lonely, need a friend or financial help. But, more so, it is about being able to give of myself.

He has given me the knowledge that love is the most important thing in life. I can express it freely with others in my walk of life, because the more you give, the more you receive. And I have truly been blessed with loving friends and family and even strangers. There is no such thing as a stranger because we are all brothers and sisters in Christ. And when God gives you all that I have received, what more is there to want?

To enjoy the beauty of His world and His people, that is truly living the meaning of life. I am so thankful that my life has been so great. To speak to Him daily, give my day to Him daily, and to read His word every day helps me to stay focused.

To be at peace and contented, that is life.

About three years after Daddy passed, Momma remarried at the age of sixty-nine. Some people might think that it would have been a bit difficult to meet a new love at such a (ahem!) mature stage of life. But in fact, Momma didn't meet someone *new*. Instead, she married a man (Terral) who just so happened to have been her classmate in the first grade! Oh, wait … it gets better. Not only had they known each other since God was born, but Terral was also Momma's first boyfriend when she was twelve years old! Granted, it is a fairly common practice for someone who is back on the market to resuscitate their little black book. But really, going all the way back to your first-grade class is stretching it a bit!

But seriously, from day one, these "lust puppies" acted like teenagers in love, nauseating everyone in their wake. I will not share any graphic details with you for fear that the mental images may scar me for life. However, I will share with you a God-given truth: I have never seen Momma happier. For that, I can only thank Terral.

Terral

> The meaning of life is something I find hard to explain. One
> thing I am sure about is that life is a very temporary thing. We are
> placed on this Earth to do God's work, and how well we do that
> work will determine our future in the hereafter.
>
> Everything we do should be done in God's name, and that
> seems to be forgotten so often. I think that if we endeavor to
> please God, we will surely reap the rewards.

I don't know how to sum up my feelings for Momma; therefore, I
won't even try. Nor do I know just how much longer I have with
Momma, so I want to take advantage of all the time I do have with
her. Having already learned from my experience with Daddy's passing, I do know that it is absolutely critical to say all of those things to
each other before it is too late. I guess that having her answer for my
book is one step toward that goal.

Queen Mary Mates

Momma and her husband, Terral, spent Christmas 2002 with me. To make their trip a bit more special, I treated them to something out of the ordinary—a night onboard the *Queen Mary* in Long Beach, California. Of course, the real reason for the treat was because I had always wanted to sleep on the ship. ("Selfish, party of one?")

We arrived at the *Queen Mary* on Christmas Eve and enjoyed a nice dinner after a tour of the ship. Afterward, I tucked in Momma and Terral for the night and left our suite to give those "lust puppies" some privacy … if you catch my drift.

To kill time, I strolled along the deserted decks for a few minutes and then found myself wandering into the chic Art Deco Observation Bar, once the ship's original first-class lounge. Seated at the bar was a young couple, Nicola and Johnnie. We quickly struck up a conversation in which I learned that they were visiting the United States from Essex, England, and were on the second leg of a three-week-long trip celebrating Johnnie's thirtieth birthday. Their trip began in Las Vegas, and after their tour of Southern California, they were ending their travels in Acapulco.

Nicola and Johnnie had been together for six years, and even though they were not married, both said that they knew they would be together for the long haul. (Yes, they *both* agreed that marriage was in their future.) But soon after marriage was mentioned, the couple began to giggle. Of course I couldn't let that go unnoticed, so I cocked a questioning eyebrow at them and waited for an explanation. They told me that even though they wanted to have children, they had chosen to put it off till the "distant future" ... like when they turned thirty! However, now that both of them had been smacked in the face by that milestone, they found that they were enjoying life so much that having children had been pushed back once again. They said that thirty-two was looking better and better.

My curiosity got the better of me and I just had to see what these two young traveling lovebirds thought was the meaning of life, so I asked.

Nicola

> Life is to be lived and enjoyed for friends and family ... family being a very big portion of life—having family and creating your own family. The biggest part of all is making the most of life and enjoying it to its full. And to find love and give love.

Johnnie

> Friends and family. Enjoyment and love. Sharing and fulfillment. Alcohol and food. Life is to be lived to the full, with no regrets. You only have one life.

Climbing the Family Tree

My brother-in-law Pat is a saint. I say this because (at the time of writing this passage) Pat has been able to successfully put up with my sister Diane for thirteen years—which is no easy task!

In all fairness, Pat has done his share of putting up with me as well. He has suffered through countless middle-of-the-night phone calls and has undergone much pain and agony from witnessing the few (OK, the many) heated discussions between Diane and me (mainly from biting his tongue during these episodes!). However, Pat's threshold for pain has really been put to the test when he has had to herd us home (against our will) after a night of partying on Bourbon Street. Yet through it all, Pat is able to remain calm (most times) and rational (always). God only knows how he does it.

Joking aside, I sincerely admire Pat for his infinite measure of patience, thoughtfulness, and generosity and his well-timed words of wisdom, which are always much appreciated. "Accept what is" has been the best piece of advice he has given me so far. I have all but tattooed this phrase on my forehead because I still forget to apply his advice when I find myself trying to change a person or situation. (I'm the first to admit that I remain a work in progress.)

I have learned so much from Pat, in more ways than he knows or that I have even been able to tell him. However, the one thing I have been able to share with him is that I consider him to be my brother ... not merely my brother-*in-law*. Calling Pat my brother is the highest honor I can think to give him.

Pat

Needless to say, this is a question that will have a different answer every time it is asked.

My meaning of life is simply living it, experiencing it, participating in it, contributing to it, sharing in the experience with others, loving, and helping others. I could go on forever. Living a good life does not take money or power or possessions.

Life is doing what you enjoy or what gives you satisfaction. Life is putting your own wants and needs as a priority without putting others too far second. You can't please everyone all the time. Set goals, and stick to them. Don't put off doing or experiencing what is important if you have the means to accomplish them. You hear the same story over and over again, "Where did the time go? I should have done this a long time ago. I would really like to do this but … I am going to start tomorrow. I just don't have the time."

Life is letting people know you have been on this Earth by helping others. It doesn't have to be monetarily. A show of concern, a kind word, or volunteering your time to help someone are just a few examples. Life is getting involved and doing.

Sharing in the experiences with family and friends are very valuable. I get as much if not more enjoyment in seeing others excited or enjoying the moment. Family and friends need to, and should always, support each other.

Life is not just existing on this Earth to take up space. Life is not just sitting or lying around and watching time and the world go by. Life is not constantly putting things off until later. Life is not constantly complaining or criticizing. Life is not looking for fault. Life is understanding that people are different and have greatly varying opinions and likes and dislikes. Listen to them, and try to understand them. Don't try to change them or try to force your views on them. Look for and acknowledge the good in people. The results will be pleasant for both. Treat everyone with respect. Many things take place daily that I don't like or agree with, but I won't let myself get all worked up about them if I can't control them. I do this to control stress, which I see as a direct detriment to one's health. It is my life, and I need to take care of my health to enjoy it fully. Sometimes things or people just are. Accept them without trying to analyze everything.

> Life is being as close as possible to my wife. To respect and be respected, to touch and hold, to share and support each other, to understand her needs and for her to understand mine. To provide all her wants, and to love her beyond my dying day.

I am very blessed to have shared time on this Earth with a group of people who are so very loving, generous, spiritual—and funnier than all heck! They are my family ... one of those southern families that is chock-full of colorful characters who you love to death one day, and then the next day you find yourself asking, *Am I really related to those people?* But as far back as I can remember, my family has always surrounded me with great love, laughter, and spirit. By example, my family has taught me to both identify with and honor my own source of humor, strength, and undying loyalty to family. We may not always acknowledge it, but the bonds of the family are thicker than the Mississippi River is muddy.

I can only speak of Momma's side of the family because I never knew Daddy's side. Momma is the youngest (living) child of a family of seven girls. To state the obvious, my Poppa (grandfather) had the pleasure to live in a house full of women. Lucky him! (Can you just imagine what he would have gone through if all of these girls had been hormonal at the same time?)

My aunts (and Momma) are true southern ladies, very polite and demure with a gentile nature like that of Miss Melanie in *Gone With the Wind.* Oh, sweet Jesus, who am I kidding? Let's face it—these ladies are complex in nature, to say the least. One minute they could be serving you coffee and cake with the sweetest spirit of southern hospitality, and in the next minute, these old broads could be kicking your butt around the block if you had been silly enough to cross them. Yet once your "whipping" was over, they would ever-so-sweetly smile again and ask whether you wanted seconds—of cake, that is.

In my eyes, Momma and her sisters have always been strong, confident women with an infinite amount of humor. Their ability to laugh freely helped them get through the many hardships they had growing up poor in the South. Even during the difficult times, these ladies learned to band together, forming a bond so strong that they could conquer anything. Their strong bond remains today.

It was not until I grew into my own skin as a southern lady that I could fully appreciate the wonderful qualities of these women. Because of them, I now more fully understand the term "steel magnolias." Can y'all give me an "Amen" to sisterhood!

Aunt Gladys

(The meaning of life is) ... what God gives me, and to appreciate what God gives me. To treat people with kindness and love. Let God take care of things for you. He's the only one that can do it.

You have to have faith and believe in God. Thank Him every day and night for what He has given you and everything He has done for you.

Love and help everyone. Do not hate. Forgive those that have done you wrong. Ask God to forgive them. Life is what you make it.

Uncle Bill

I have learned so much in life from those that walked before me, with God! First of all, let's thank the Lord that we are all together and still alive. Our dreams may still come true: to survive and go bravely on. Any wrongs that we have done, God forgives us.

Thank you, Lord, for helping my mate every day.

Aunt Millie

To serve God is the most meaningful thing in my life. Family, my children, my sisters are important to me. To appreciate the love we receive from family. And anticipating the new life that God offers in the autumn of my life.

Agnes

> To live the best I know how. Be kind and of service to others. To keep my eyes on Jesus and let him lead me on this journey of life.

Oscar

> Life is a treasure that God has given me. I am so thankful for those that love me and so thankful for those that I love. God bless you for allowing me to be a part of your book.

Then there is (second) Cousin Theresa, the epitome of a mature, church-going southern lady. She faithfully attends mass every Sunday, arriving an hour early to socialize (and to make sure no one sits in her spot). Church is the perfect place for Cousin Theresa to wear her stylish hats, which she designs and sews on her own. To her credit, she has made well over a hundred hats.

Cousin Theresa is also a kind and generous person, willing to give you the shirt off her back. But, darlin', if you ever cross her, she will first say a prayer for you and then proceed to kick your butt around the block a few times until you beg for mercy! (I guess she learned this from my aunts.)

To this day, I have yet to see Cousin Theresa bare faced, meaning that she always wears makeup. I guess being the old-fashioned southern lady that she is, Cousin Theresa follows the rule that a lady should never walk out of the house without first having put on her "face." Her makeup, always flawlessly applied with a graceful hand, displays her signature look of a face covered in sweet-smelling alabaster powder and cheeks accented with two rosy dots. The finishing touch is her crimson-colored lips, which leave an imprint on your cheek long after the day is done.

If I live to be a hundred, I don't think that I will ever meet anyone who comes close to being the character that is Cousin Theresa. She is one of those rare people in life who will be forever remembered by all who meet her. Like her lipstick on your cheek, her infectious smile and loving spirit leave a permanent mark on your heart.

Cousin Theresa

> Life is a great thing, girl, especially when you talk with a lot of great friends. It's a great thing to be an American. God gave me a wonderful mother. I had a wonderful life. God gave me the man I love. I prayed to God for him, and He gave him to me ... married fifty-four years ... and God has taken him from me; it's eleven years he's passed.
>
> I could not have asked for a better life. It's so good to be alive and to have all the conveniences that God has given us. God is so good and I thank Him every day for what He gives me, what He takes away, and what He leaves me.

◆   ◆   ◆

Elaine and Susan are my cousins, and I cannot talk about one without the other because the bond between these two gals is closer to being that of best friends or even sisters. They have been able to transcend the typical relationship between cousins (which in most families is either distant or nonexistent) to become an integral part of each other's lives.

When I was growing up, I always studied these two lovely ladies with a sense of wonder. Mostly I wondered how I could be related to such vivacious, free-spirited women when my own reserved nature was in such extreme contrast. How did they come to possess such a sense of freedom, such a sense of self? Had I inherited any of these characteristics? In other words, if there are traits that are shared throughout a family tree, were any seedlings of Susan and Elaine's effervescence laying dormant somewhere in me? As a child, I didn't know how genetics worked, so I remained content to just enjoy my time around them.

I have lived away from Susan and Elaine for over twenty years, yet I can be in their presence today and still feel the same sense of awe and wonder that I felt as a child. These days, though, I wonder whether I possess some of the same genes that will allow me to age as gracefully as these two fabulous women. I hope so.

Elaine

To appreciate everything in life, even things you don't have and may wish for. Also, to understand that if there is something you thought was so important that it would make your life better if you had it, isn't necessarily so. Most importantly, to appreciate the smallest things in life because they are definitely the most rewarding. If there is something in life you want to do, do it. Don't just wish it, because you have a fifty-fifty chance of getting what you want.

Susan

Living … learning … laughing the best I can at all times. Being an alcoholic and addict has been a growth experience in more ways than one. Faith in God is the best treasure I have received in life. Through all my trials and tribulations, and to have come out on the other side with a God that loves me no matter what. Generosity with your possessions, your time, and yourself is, and always will be, important.

Family is everywhere. Look around and find yourself one if you are not fortunate to have one of your own. There are people in need of love; find them and you find out about yourself. Children … always be one and inspire, encourage, and teach as many children as you can.

◆   ◆   ◆

I wasn't a very good aunt to the "kids" of the family while they were growing up—although I really shouldn't call them kids any longer because they range in ages from eighteen to twenty-eight. God, are they getting old or what? And they are the only ones getting old, thank you very much!

I moved to California when the oldest kids were only about two years old, and I totally missed the births of the last three kids. Living so far away, I also missed out on opportunities to attend birthday parties, school functions, and just about all family gatherings. It's not that I never saw my nieces and nephews, but our time together was rare and all too brief. Even though I was kept abreast of their lives through the countless stories from their parents, it was never the same as being there in person.

From day one, I knew that I was going to pay a price for living so far away from them. Therefore, I made a promise to myself long ago that I would make a concerted effort to have a meaningful relationship with each of them once they were older. Since I had missed their baby days and *wanted* to miss their teenaged "punk" stage (just kidding!), my plan was to approach them when they reached their early twenties and tell them of my desire for a closer relationship. I chose that age because they would be beyond their teenage years and yet, hopefully, not yet marrying and having babies.

So far, I have approached four of the five kids with the same declaration—"I want to begin a relationship with you"—and offered up the same basic game plan to all. As for the fifth and final "kid," I'm waiting for just the right time to corner her!

Let me quickly address the hecklers in the crowd: no, not one of them groaned in despair at hearing that I wanted to start a *relationship* (at least not in front of me). I had determined that the best way to kick off each getting-to-know-you adventure was by having a face-to-face conversation so that I could explain what the heck I was up to. Considering that they played a crucial role in this adventure, I thought it only fitting they should know the full story.

My conversation with each of them covered several bases. First, I started by taking responsibility for my absence from their childhood, admitting that I could have been more involved in their lives. Then I apologized for having missed so many special moments of their youth, and I told them that I had been bothered for some time by the distance in our relationship caused by my absence. Finally, I explained that I wanted to make it right. It was my desire to get to know them beyond the roles of aunt and niece/nephew and to be more like friends than distant relatives.

Each conversation ended awkwardly as I asked, "Do you want to start a relationship with me?" In their own ways, they all said yes (thank God!). Of course, since they were held captive until they listened to my entire spiel, it was possible that they only agreed just to get me to shut up. But since they could never prove in a court of law that they were held hostage, I'm just focusing on taking the time to develop these relationships and enjoying the adventure.

From reading their answers, I think they'll find that life has in store a little adventure for each of them to enjoy.

Eric

> ... knowing that somewhere among the vast emptiness of the Earth and space, there is something or someone watching, planning, and guiding humans toward their dreams, whether the dreams are good or bad. The faith that the human race has for that something up there makes life meaningful. So, I like to say, "Why is life meaningful?" instead of "What is the meaning of life?" Because the fact is, all humans have a different meaning of life, which makes the question "What is the meaning of life?" useless. It is because all humans find life meaningful that makes breathing, talking, loving, and living meaningful enough not to ask "What is the meaning of life?"

Lauren

> The meaning of life? An age-old question with no answer. It's quite possible that there is no meaning—that God put us here to watch us, much like children who have ant farms. It's a possibil-

ity. However, I personally think that there is much more to life. I believe in eternal life and in reincarnation, and the meaning of life on Earth is to help the spirit grow.

Everybody is sent to Earth with a special mission, unbeknownst to them. This mission can be anything but usually involves helping other people by using the special and unique talents that they possess. In doing/completing this mission, both the person and the people they help are given the opportunity to grow spiritually. Therefore, when they die, their spirit lives on but has expanded and will be given future opportunities for further growth. In this way, life is simply a means through which spirits may grow and should, therefore, be spent trying to maximize this growth.

Adam

I believe that you should enjoy life to the fullest, and make every day count as if it was your last. My mantra (which I live by) is *carpe diem*, "seize the day." On the other hand, you should also leave your mark on the world. Doing someone a favor from time to time can change that person's life dramatically. Living every day like it is your last and impacting someone's life will enrich your soul as well as give your life meaning.

Brian

To pass on your genes. To pass on your knowledge, joy, and love to others to enhance their lives. And if nothing else, to laugh. You must always laugh.

God Bless the Child

My niece Caroline (the last "kid") entered the world with a special spark in her soul. My other niece and nephews have their own unique spark as well, but I'm singling out Caroline because several years ago she uttered words to her mom that I have lived by ever since.

Many years ago my sister, Tina, took skiing her three children—Brian, seventeen; Lauren, fourteen; and Caroline, around eight at the time. One day while skiing, Caroline's siblings decided to attempt a very difficult run. Knowing the advanced athletic talent of these two, I would bet the farm that it was one of the most difficult runs on the mountain. Not to be left behind, Caroline followed in their tracks with her own competitive nature in tow.

Once Caroline made it safely down the treacherous slope, all limbs in tact, my sister lauded her with praise and amazement.

"Are you OK? Were you scared?" my sister anxiously asked.

After a few minutes of taking in this praise and glory for a job well done, Caroline humbly looked up at her Mom and shrugged. "It's all in what you think it is."

I was blown away when I learned that such courageous and profound words came out of her little mouth. I found Caroline's words to be so inspirational that I wrote them on a piece of paper, taped the paper to the wall of my office, and read it almost every day for ten years. As a salesperson, I found the words to be very helpful in dealing with rejection.

Many years have passed since Caroline uttered those profound words. In fact, she doesn't even remember saying them. (That happens with age!) However, I have kept her words close to my heart and have used them whenever I get stuck in life, like when I get afraid of taking a step forward. For me, her words continue to put life into perspective and help me walk through to the other side of fear.

Caroline

It's all in what you think it is.

I will never have children of my own, and I'm OK with that. What I'm not OK with, however, is sitting by and not reaching out to children in need.

Over the years, I've attempted to offer a helping hand to children by volunteering as a Big Sister and as a juvenile detention ministry counselor—both challenging but very rewarding experiences. Unfortunately, at that time I was unable to strike a good balance with my work schedule and ended up not having the quality time to devote to these programs. Fortunately, since my new chapter in life afforded me time away from work, I started volunteering again, this time at a local children's hospital.

To further satisfy my desire to help children, I am blessed with the ability to sponsor three children from the Christian Children's Fund (CCF) organization. I have known Fernanda (Brazil) then fourteen, and Luis (Bolivia) thirteen, since 1999; Veronica (Kenya) ten, joined our little family in 2002. We exchange letters several times a year and learn a bit more about the other each time.

It's always such a thrill to open my mailbox and see a letter from one of them. Whether the letter is about family, school, work, friends, or hobbies, it's so rewarding to learn more about these young people and their daily lives.

My dream for the future, in addition to adding more children to the fold, is to take these relationships to the next level, meaning that I hope one day to meet them face-to-face. Therefore, *when* (positive affirmation) the sale of this book provides the extra "coin," my butt will be on an airplane to visit the children faster than you can say "passport, please."

These children play a powerful role in my life by serving as reminders that the world is filled, not with strangers, but with loving brothers and sisters I have yet to meet. And if you haven't already guessed, I do believe that I am my brother's keeper.

Veronica

> The meaning of life—it is to be contented with what you have.

Luis

> If somebody doesn't know the meaning of life, he or she doesn't know why she or he is living. Life for me is the most exciting experience that one can have.

Fernanda

> As to what life means to me, it is something sublime and wonderful where God gives us opportunities of living, loving, and being happy. It is enough to believe and struggle for our goals, because living is winning.

Bella Italia

Now that I had obtained answers to my question from most of my family and longtime friends, I asked myself *who else has touched my heart?* My mind quickly answered this question by serving up memories of my very first trip to Italy in 2001.

I remember being so excited about going to Italy that it didn't bother me that I was going alone. But for some nagging reason, I sensed that traveling alone on this trip was not a good idea. Therefore, I ended up joining a bus tour—another "first" for me. I soon learned that on a bus trip, one is rarely alone when surrounded by forty-eight fellow travelers. (I wondered whether this was going to be a case of "be careful what you wish for"!)

My love affair with Italy began on that trip. (Italy had me at "ciao"!) My two-week trip had me covering a great deal of the country, including Rome, Florence, Pisa, Siena, Assisi, Milan, Venice, Sorrento, and the island of Capri. From the moment I boarded the bus, sparks of affection ignited in my heart and flamed even brighter each day as I watched the beautiful countryside unfold outside my window. Everywhere I looked, Italy displayed her grace and beauty, and my bond with her grew stronger as we traveled. The more I was exposed to the fabulous art and architecture, food and wine, and loving spirit of the Italian people, the more I became hopelessly enchanted. Yet I learned early on that my love for Italy wouldn't be the only bond I would forge on this trip.

On the second day of my trip, this busload of strangers and I were thrust into a situation far beyond what anyone could imagine. You see, it was on the second day of our trip that 9/11 happened. It didn't matter in which country these travelers lived; that horrific event hit everyone equally hard and brought us closer together than anything else could have possibly accomplished. Our first instinct was to turn to one another to console and be consoled, and after the initial shock lessened, we silently vowed to dedicate the rest of our trip to those souls who were making another sort of journey that day.

Life for me changed on that sad day, much as it had for everyone else in the world. Being without family or friends in a foreign country during such an awful time brought about painful feelings of home-sickness, something I had never felt before. It was the first time in my life that I heard myself say, "I just need to be back on U.S. soil. Just get me back home." In fact, as odd as it sounds, it also was the first time that I had ever stated aloud how much I loved America and appreciated the honor of being a citizen. I know I had always felt this way, but never before had I said it aloud with tears and such convic-tion. One could say that on this trip, I also formed a closer bond with America.

One of the many wonderful people I met on this bus trip was a lovely woman from Louisville, Kentucky. She wants to be known as "CGE." To get the true picture of this little firecracker, picture a petite blond, decades past the age of thirtysomething, yet still looking darn good for her place in life! Maybe it was her heavy southern drawl, her protective nature, her adorable smile, or her bigger-than-she-is-tall-sized heart that had me immediately feeling comforted. Whatever it was, I can still feel her presence in my heart.

CGE was one of several people I met in Italy who kept a watchful eye over my whereabouts. I didn't take offense to this motherly atten-tion (even though I was fortysomething at the time), nor did I ques-tion it. I merely lapped up the generosity and kindness I was shown.

I was able to spend time with CGE during our two-week trip, but it still wasn't enough to get to know her as well as I would have liked. I was afforded only a brief taste of her loving energy, yet my moments with her have forever been seared into my heart. I only hope that somehow she is still keeping an eye out for me.

CGE

> For me, life is a journey from our birth to our death. To me, at this stage of my life it is a spiritual journey. I believe life was given to me as a gift by God, who is Love. Loving is what He wants us to do on this journey. We do this by sharing with others the gifts and talents we were given. This is no easy task, this loving others.
>
> Our human nature is such that we tend to be selfish and filled with pride, and also filled with many other worldly vices. In times of challenge and crisis, He promised to walk with us and even carry us if necessary. I believe He does this through His angels here on Earth—you and me. If we truly love and follow His way, we will have the best of all—"eternal life." That is His promise.
>
> My favorite quote in the Bible is "Eye has not seen, ear has not heard what God has made ready for those who love him." (Corinthians)

After being set free from my job in October 2002, I returned to my beloved Italy the following January to celebrate the new chapter of my life and my newfound freedom.

I must confess that my love for Italy is so strong that I'm beginning to think that I must have lived there in a past life. But for my current incarnation, I was happy just to have another opportunity to revisit this magnificent place.

For my second rendezvous with Italy, I spent two weeks in Tuscany—mainly Florence. There I met several wonderful people, all so willing to be a part of my book family.

Although I struggled a bit with the language barrier each time, the effort was worthwhile. I was rewarded with and inspired by people's warmth, friendliness, and overall love of life. With every encounter, I was reminded that we have far more things in common with each other than we have differences. Even though I have always believed this on some level, it was not until I experienced people in other parts of the world that I believed it on a more soulful level.

The lovely Ristorante Corsini was located a few steps from my pensione in Florence, making it a convenient spot to begin the night's activities and toast my arrival.

Massimo, the bartender, was the first cute guy I saw in the city, and he blushed when I told him so. When he heard that it was my first night in his lovely city, he poured me a very healthy glass of wine to celebrate my arrival—yet another example of the gracious hospitality and loving spirit of the Italian people.

Soon after the introductions were over, I asked him to be a part of my book. Of course, some people might accuse me of asking him to be in my book only because I thought he was cute.... (Do you really think I'm going to respond to that?)

Massimo

Satisfy my curiosity. I am curious about everything.

I was happy to have Massimo's answer, but my reaction to his answer was surprisingly less than positive. For some unknown reason, it left me feeling a bit annoyed. *Satisfy my curiosity? Quit telling me what to do!* (Wow! Where did that come from?) As crazy as it sounds, it felt as though his words were purposely directed at me, as if they were ordering me to do something. To say the least, I got a bit perturbed, as I always do when I think someone is trying to order me about (hence the snippy thoughts).

I didn't understand why I had interpreted his words that way. For goodness sake, his words were for him, not me. But his words had indeed struck a nerve in me, despite knowing that whatever had caused my reaction had nothing to do with Massimo. *It is never about the other person.* Thankfully, in that moment, I had enough reserve to keep my thoughts to myself.

Only after much reflection, and several rewrites of this section, was I able to get to the truth behind my reaction. As best as I can understand it, I think Massimo's answer ignited a long-standing internal struggle in me between Ego and Spirit. Whereas Ego tries to convince me that I am not deserving or worthy of anything good and that I should be fearful of everything, Spirit counteracts by offering loving guidance and encouragement to believe in myself. The struggle ensues when Ego fights to gain control of a situation, which is exactly what happened with my reaction to Massimo's answer. Spirit had actually delivered a wonderful message—*satisfy my curiosity*—reminding me to continue the pursuit of my dreams and to never revert back to that scared child I had once been. But Ego was having none of that. Before Spirit's words even had time to register in my consciousness, Ego diverted my attention with its scream of protest: *quit telling me what to do!*

As I now understand more of what happened in that moment, I know that I was left feeling annoyed not because of the answer itself but because in that moment I had decided to let Ego have the last word. It was like I had given in to the tantrum of a two-year-old, which is never a good idea. When I realized this, I was annoyed with myself because I knew better.

Fortunately these days, I listen to Spirit more than ever. But when I do suffer a lapse, I can decipher a less-than-positive reaction with much more ease and in far less time. Also, I have since learned a shortcut to reaching the truth. I merely ask myself one question: *in this moment, am I living in Ego or in Spirit?* It works wonders.

After a long night of touring Florence, the restaurant was a good place to return to for a nightcap. Within minutes of arriving, I was welcomed with gracious hospitality by owner Gino. I spent only a few minutes talking with him yet I could tell that he not only possessed a very serious side when it came to his business, but that he was also very warm and fun-loving. The fact that he sang along to every Frank Sinatra song that played in the background was all the evidence I needed.

The hour was late (according to my jet-lagged body) but there still remained in the restaurant a dozen or so local patrons. I guess it was my pathetic attempts to converse with them in Italian that gave me away to being an American. But everyone had so much fun laughing at each other's translation foibles that we decided to join tables. Through the laughter and despite the language barrier, somehow we were able to understand each other.

What happened next I only blame on Frank Sinatra and Gino's passionate singing of *New York, New York.* Within seconds of recognizing the song, everyone sprung out of their chairs and began dancing. Mind you, there was no formal dance floor. In fact, one of the waiters later divulged the fact that Gino had never before allowed dancing in his restaurant.

Why had Gino allowed dancing that night? Who knows. Maybe it was Frank Sinatra's spirit working its magic. Or just maybe it was the contagious spirit that occurs when human beings reach out to each other. I like to think it's both.

Gino

L'amore!

Gino said that his answer meant more than just making love or being in love but that one should feel love for everything—life, water, work. Love absolutely everything.

If memory serves, it was in Roberto's ristorante, La Sagrestia, where I fell in love with *ribollita,* a traditional Tuscan soup made by adding bread to leftover vegetable soup (minestrone). Now that may not sound too appetizing, but I would bet the farm that you would like it.

Granted, I tried *ribollita* on a cold winter's day in Florence, so anything hot would have been great. The combination of the hot soup and Roberto's warm nature (and good looks!) took the chill off my bones. Of course the *vino rosso* did its part as well.

What I loved about Roberto was the fact that when he saw me writing in my journal, he was not afraid to walk over to my table and express his curiosity. Sure, the myth of the assertive Italian male may be true, but if I had to choose between a man who is afraid of his own shadow—meaning a man who lacks the courage to walk up to a woman to even say hi—and an assertive Italian man, well, heck, *ciao bello!* Give me the Italian male any day of the week. For Italians, love is always in the air.

Roberto

> In life, it is very important to be sincere, respect all people, be honest, and to live life every day thoughtfully because life is the most beautiful thing in the world.

Luigi was dining at a nearby table at Il Cantastorie Ristorante, and as we enjoyed the restaurant's entertainment, a conversation ignited. We had so much fun speaking with each other. While Luigi enjoyed practicing his English, I had fun fumbling through my limited Italian. We merely laughed at each other's blunders and continued to navigate our way through a meaningful and insightful conversation about life.

Luigi agreed to be in my book so long as he could dictate his answer to me, and I was happy to oblige. Within just a few minutes into the dictation, it became apparent that Luigi was reciting part of my own personal philosophy. I lived miles away and worlds apart, yet I was brought together with someone who shared my views on life. I love when that happens.

The similarity of our beliefs, and the fact that Luigi had even used the same phrases and terminology that I would have chosen, simply amazed me. As I continued to write down his words, I could only smile and nod in agreement.

Once again, there are no accidents in life. I believe that the reason Luigi and I began conversing in the first place was because we intuitively or subconsciously "recognized" the other as being on the same path. *We are not alone.*

Luigi

> Dreaming is to have one dream, and don't stop to wish your dream. Everyday life often gets us far from our dream, and makes us less sensitive to the signs of what destiny sends to us: The Way. I think that we receive the signs for finding the way of our wish. We must not lose the ability to listen or see this message.
>
> I think that when you really want something, the universe works with you, because your wish becomes true. The price is sometimes a big sacrifice.

Another great place that was just steps from my pensione was the beautiful Hotel Excelsior.

Upon entering the hotel's lounge, I was greeted by Sergio, who I cannot describe as a regular waiter because he was more like the lounge's maitre d'. His air of relaxed authority convinced patrons that he was in total control of that area of the hotel.

After taking much care to seat me (away from any smokers, thank you very much), Sergio took my order, quickly delivered my drink—a B&B—and then discreetly kept an eye on my needs. Of that night, there is no more to tell.

Two weeks later, on my last night in Florence, I returned to the Hotel Excelsior for an *arrivederci* toast to Italy. Immediately recognizing me, Sergio greeted me ever so warmly and seated me at a nice table. In taking my drink order, Sergio asked, "Would you like a B&B?" Let me remind you that it was B&B I had ordered on my first visit to the hotel—some fourteen days prior. For Sergio to remember my drink order after so much time had passed simply amazed me. In my mind, he was someone who was absolutely great at his job. I also envied his memory.

It was a Saturday night, and the lounge filled up quickly. Seating became scarcer by the minute. Knowing that I was alone, Sergio asked whether he could seat a few Italian ladies at my table. Now, honestly, had Sergio put a few Italian men at my table, I would have French-kissed him right then and there! But considering the fact that I love to people-watch, especially in a foreign country, it was a perfect opportunity to watch the night's merriment unfolding before me.

Sergio seated the ladies at my table, introducing me as his American friend. The ladies and I briefly exchanged pleasantries as best we could considering the language barrier and then proceeded to enjoy the band. After listening to most of the band's first set, I couldn't help but notice that all of the songs were American. I could somewhat forgive that aspect of the entertainment, but I was more disappointed that the songs were being sung in English. Mind you, I didn't travel all the way to Italy to have English sung in my ears. Furthermore, since I had spent many grueling weeks prior to my trip learning (how not to butcher) the Italian language, I wanted to hear Italian songs sung in Italian.

When traveling to a foreign country, I don't want my surroundings to be exactly like home. In fact, the very reason I travel outside of the States is so that I can be fully immersed in different cultures, of which music and language play a big part.

After a few more songs were performed, I couldn't hold back any longer. I asked the ladies at the table whether the band's performance was fairly typical for the area. To their affirmative reply, I offered my thanks with a disappointed sigh.

After playing several songs back-to-back, the band paused a few minutes, and then started up again. To my surprise, they started performing a beautiful Italian song—in Italian.

As soon as I noticed the change in music, I lifted my head from my journal and beamed a smile at the ladies as if to say, *Oh, that's much better.* They nodded in agreement, but their mischievous Cheshire cat grins told me that they were up to something. Sure enough, I was right. Come to find out, one of the ladies had told Sergio of my disappointment over the music and asked him to request the band to play a special Italian song (just for me), with specific instructions for it to be sung in Italian. How sweet was that?

This simple, sweet gesture broke the ice with the ladies, and from that moment on, we plunged into a lovely conversation, which of course included them taking part in my book.

One of the ladies (Betty) asked what I thought of Florence. Well, that was a mistake, because I went on and on about how much I had fallen in love with her city. I think I broke the world's record for the number of times one can say the word *bella*. While listening to my rambling, Betty began writing something on a piece of paper, which she then handed to me. It was her address! She told me that *when* I returned to Florence, I had a place to stay. Do I love Italians or what? Ciao bella!

As the night progressed, I continued to discreetly watch the ladies at my table as they enjoyed receiving the well-deserved attention from several marauding males. I couldn't help but compare the shenanigans of the night to those that take place on such a night in the States.

My observations, although unscientific in their collection, confirmed that the search for *amore* is pretty much the same worldwide. All of the same tricks of the trade are used; the same winks, smiles, and "costumes" are displayed by the hopeful wanting to meet Mr. or Ms. Right.

I guess it could have been comforting to witness single people in Florence having just as hard of a time meeting the opposite sex, as do Americans; something along the lines of misery loves company. But it only made my heart ache to know that on this night, so many wonderful people—here in Florence and around the world—would go home feeling lonely and unloved.

Sergio

> For me, what is the most important thing of life is being honest and sincere with my fellow man and with my family.

Betty

To know my soul, the demon, my shadow, the limit.

Cristina

The most important thing in life is love, the spring for energy of life, the sun that warms the heart and the hook for the sky.

Daniela

A large love and sole true source of maintenance for life. And the love that moves the sun and all the other stars.

Luciana

A great love, such passion. To live without limits.

Momma Cries Out

I am nothing like my mother. I have said this my entire life. (Yes, snickering is allowed!) But now that I'm older—I mean wiser—I think maybe it is because of our many similarities that our bond has grown stronger every day.

Never was this more obvious to me than when I traveled to Positano, Italy, in August 2003.

I arrived in Positano on a Thursday (keep this day in mind). After checking into my pensione around noon, I got my bearings and within minutes was out the door wandering through the charming little village.

I walked the quaint, narrow streets for only a short time when the strangest feeling washed over me. It felt like an enormous wave of sadness had crashed on top of me, lasting for several minutes. When the wave receded, I felt shaken and disoriented both physically and emotionally. I know it sounds a bit dramatic, but in that moment, I felt as though I could have started crying, right there on the street. It was an awful feeling.

Now, let me quickly discount the obvious female disclaimers: it was neither "that time of the month," nor was it a full moon or anything as logical as that.

In the wake of the wave, the only debris left behind was one thought: *I want to go home.*

By getting to this point in my book, I think you know how much I love Italy so you can imagine how weird it was for me to want to leave. Typically, the very idea of leaving my beloved Italy, especially on the same day that I arrived, *never* would have entered my mind! On the contrary, I'm usually thinking: *what would it take to stay even longer?*

Regardless of how confusing it was to want to leave Italy, I didn't poo-poo any of the thoughts and feelings I was experiencing. I firmly believed that it was all happening for a reason. But what was the reason? Why was I feeling so sad? Why did I want to go home?

The next day, Friday, I called to check in with my sister Diane, as I always do when traveling, no matter where I am in the world. I thought I had correctly figured out the time difference between Italy and New Orleans, but when she didn't answer, I just left a message and didn't give it a second thought.

Diane is faithful about returning my calls, especially when I'm out traveling, but this time she didn't call back. Oddly enough, I didn't think much about it and merely finished the rest of my week in Positano. However, throughout the week, I still experienced strong bouts of sadness.

The day of my departure arrived. During a layover in Chicago, I again called Diane to check in with her. Well, darlin', was I in for a surprising conversation or what?

Diane proceeded to explain that on the day I arrived in Positano, Thursday—also the same day I began feeling sad and wanting to go home—Momma had suffered a stroke. Yes, a stroke!

I stood in the middle of Chicago O'Hare airport unable to grasp this reality. My fingers squeezed the telephone receiver tighter with every labored breath. Yet through the shock of it all, I suddenly understood everything that had happened to me.

I believe that the reason I had felt such a strong feeling of sadness when I arrived in Positano was because I had actually received Momma's cry for help. Both happened on the same day. I later learned that after her stroke, Momma and Diane had struggled the entire week trying to decide whether they should call me home. In my mind, that answered the question as to why the desire to return home had persisted throughout my entire vacation. Their strong thoughts about calling me home had reached out and tugged at my psyche. It all made sense.

Although it was indeed awful to learn of Momma's stroke, hearing the details and the timeline of the events certainly solved the mystery behind my unusual emotional experience.

This experience served to underscore a few of my existing beliefs. My first belief is that when I totally accept and embrace the moment, the truth of the moment is revealed. Secondly, I know that by listening to Spirit, I am given the knowledge to connect the dots of my life and receive confirmation once again that things happen for a reason. Lastly, I believe that the peace I enjoy in life comes from knowing that no matter the physical distance between Momma and me, nothing can weaken the profound connection we share.

A few days after returning home from Italy, I was back on an airplane heading to Momma's side. I stayed with her for three weeks straight (which was easy to do since I was still unemployed).

During my stay, my entire family—brothers, sisters, cousins, aunts, and uncles—pitched in to help Momma recover. Some cooked. Some provided emotional comfort. Others kept her laughing. My part in this recovery effort was to play the role of Nurse Ratched (the stern nurse from *One Flew Over the Cuckoo's Nest)*. My mission was to whip Momma back into physical and emotional shape.

Momma was indeed blessed to have such a strong support system, and the blessings continued with the addition of her team of professional caretakers, who worked the hardest of all. Although quite skilled in their respective fields, each of them also carried in their bag of tricks an abundant supply of warmth, humor, and compassion.

If you ever want to meet the epitome of a southern gentleman and full-fledged Cajun, then look up Andre, Momma's occupational therapist. Some of his co-workers affectionately call him "Crazy Andre." After spending only a few minutes with him, I guessed that his nickname was due to his great sense of humor and larger-than-life personality.

After watching Andre work tirelessly with Momma day after day, I would venture to say that he taps into a higher spirit while he works. The loving energy and compassion he showed Momma went well beyond the call of duty.

It was an honor to meet Andre, and I will forever be inspired by his *joie de vivre*.

Andre

> Life, as defined by myself, encompasses tangible, as well as abstract variables. Things of nature, which are both visible and invisible, provide solace and comfort. People and their behaviors, be they pleasing or abrasive, provide a component of interaction. Faith in a power greater than me offers sanity.
>
> These variables, when combined along with my "laissez-faire" attitude, allow me to enjoy one of the most blessed privileges a breathing mammal can have: Life.
>
> In summation, being outdoors, able to see, hear, and feel the environment surrounding me is what I live for. Anything that comes my way, be it family, friends, or money is all "lagniappe," that is, an added bonus.

For the first month after Momma's stroke, nurse practitioner Connie visited twice a week to record Momma's vital signs and help take care of her personal needs. Connie's presence was a welcomed gift because when she entered the room, you could feel her joy and happiness. I don't say this lightly. Although there are many happy people who cross my path, only a rare few exude such a luminous glow.

I believe that Connie's glow of happiness stems from her knowing that she has in life what she has always wanted—a great husband and children—and she gratefully acknowledges the blessing of it all. Connie doesn't boast about her abundant life; she wears her happiness proudly, yet humbly. That in itself is a great gift.

Connie

Happiness. Being happy with who you are and who you are with. My two sons and grandchild. My husband. All of this is my life. Without them, I don't think I would have a life.

"Nurse Ratched"

I don't have to wait until I'm at death's door to know that life is all about love. There is absolutely nothing more important. I am not talking about just the concept of love, but rather the conscious practice of loving. For me to be able to truly honor the gift of love, it is vital that I continue to learn how to be better at giving my love, and as importantly, be better at receiving love from others. This continuing process is what gives meaning to my life and brings me closer to the Source.

The Best Job in the World

"Hello, my name is Louise, and I am a chocoholic."

Although this is not very far from the truth, I do my best to curb my appetite for the smooth, lush, scrumptious taste of chocolate—and I know that I'm not alone. I mean really, what self-respecting woman has not polished off a box (or bag) of these delectable morsels during a time of need? Yes, some men are equally guilty. Even if you haven't raised your hand, I'm sure you've had the pleasure of popping a few too many chocolates every now and then. And that's OK. Chocolate is a good thing.

I think the only time you really have to worry about your chocolate intake is when you are too embarrassed to tell your closest friend the truth about just how much chocolate you ate the night before. Or when after a chocolate binge, you wake up the next morning with a chocolate smear on your face. For those of us who are guilty on both counts, you are not alone. Maybe there is a crisis hotline for us out there.

If I were to name the most perfect job on Earth—other than being George Clooney's massage therapist—it would be a job where I had free chocolates at my fingertips every second of the day. One night at dinner, I met a man who had such an enviable job.

His name was Art, and when he told me that he worked for a candy company, I melted into a state of awe and hung on his every word. Had I listened so intently because I was I riveted by his story of becoming a candy man? Well, OK, that's a possibility. But the truth would be closer to the fact that I was hoping he was handing out free samples.

Art and I had a wonderful conversation that, thankfully, turned "real" in a short period of time. Not that I don't enjoy talking about chocolate, but it was far more interesting learning that Art is one of those enlightened souls who learns from past experiences.

Art

> First and foremost: do no harm. I fully realize where the quote originates, but I don't believe it applies, or should apply, only to the medical profession.
>
> We have been given the gift of life. And it is a gift to make a positive impression on our fellow man. We have an obligation to protect and preserve the sanctity of life; to do less is a crime against humanity.
>
> We must be productive, honest, and live up to our societal obligations. In so doing, life's meaning will be evident and obvious. Happiness and peace will follow, and the "feared" end death will merely be a part of life—albeit the end of this life, and hopefully the beginning of another. The End!

Boy Meets Girl

My relationship with Dave began in typical fashion: Boy sees girl. Girl is oblivious to boy. Girl's gal pal wants boy instead. Boy not going for that. Boy still wants first girl. Girl then catches on. Girl says to boy, "Let's be friends." Boy sighs, "Here we go again."

This isn't quite the storybook romance we all want to hear, but there you have it. However, I'm happy to say that this story doesn't end in typical fashion. Even though I countered Dave's flattering approach with the dreaded line of "let's be friends," Dave didn't cop an attitude and toss me aside like a hot potato (unlike some men faced with this situation). Instead, he agreed to be my friend.

Although I have made many attempts to tell him, I'm not sure if Dave really knows just how much I admire him for accepting my friendship. It's due much to Dave's openness and acceptance of reality that our friendship continues.

As to my thoughts about Dave's continued search, I sincerely hope that the next time I ask Dave this question, he will have found his answer. But just to be safe, maybe I will wait a while and give him some time before asking again … like when we're about eighty years old!

David

> I have been asking myself the same question all of my life. In fact, that is what I am trying to figure out right now in my current escapade. Perhaps, it is merely answering that question itself. Once it is answered, is the game over, and are the lights shut off?

Is it finding happiness, self-fulfillment, or love? I am still searching. Is it not about one's self? If it is about selfless help to others, I
suppose I will not pass the test with flying colors. In my current
state of life, I suppose the meaning is elusive and changing. I
think I am getting a little wiser and mellowing as my hair grays.

Enough waxing philosophy … I don't follow a role model; I
have never really looked for one. I think part of the meaning is to
treat others as I would like to be treated—that is, with honesty
and respect. That qualification does, however, have its drawbacks,
as it leads to being judgmental, and I definitely don't like being
judged. Maybe it is resolving these little contradictions.

The other aspect is finding what I love to do, and using my
talents and abilities to that end. My current search lies in that
aspect—that is, what do I love to do?

To sum up these random thoughts … if I really knew what
the meaning of life was, I would be pursuing it with vigor. For
now, I am still searching for the answer.

A Man-Made Lake, a God-Given Blessing

By now, you already know that I believe there are no accidents in life and that everything happens for a reason. I know that this concept probably has been debated since the beginning of time, much like the topic of this book. But without delving too deeply into it, I think there are two camps of believers: those who think that events in life are the result of random chaos, and the others (like me), who believe that everything happens for a reason.

Although I try to stay open to the opinions of those other thinkers, I can only state that on most days of my life, an event will occur to back up my belief. Now, if others can say the same for their argument, well then, long live the debate.

As a side note, if you're not exactly sure which side of this debate you fall on, let me offer an easy test. First, sit in a quiet place where you won't be disturbed. Take a few deep-cleansing breaths, and begin to focus on how you're feeling inside.

Next, think upon these two concepts: The first concept suggests that everything happens in your life without rhyme or reason—purely random events. The second concept proposes that there are higher reasons behind the events that happen in your life.

Now, take time to think upon each concept until you can make an argument for either side. Then, focus on your inner feelings as you ponder both concepts.

The final step: ask yourself which concept promoted a feeling of inner peace. There's your answer.

On a hot summer evening, I went to Waters Restaurant. It remains a favorite of mine because it sits on the edge of a man-made lake that also serves as a duck pond and quasi-bird sanctuary. For several reasons, be it physiological, astrological, or psychological, I have to be near water whenever possible. I especially love being around "big water"—aka, my ocean, the Pacific. But I digress.

While sitting on the waterfront patio, my attention was drawn to an older couple sitting at the next table. For the life of me, I cannot adequately describe the energy that radiated from this couple other than to say that it was pure love. From the expressions on their faces, this couple seemed to be at peace with life and thrilled to be together. They didn't speak much but merely looked across the water, enjoying the other's company.

A few minutes passed when I saw the woman scooting her chair closer to the gentleman (not that I was spying on them or anything). Then, they exchanged a lingering kiss, gentle and filled with meaning. To see the way in which these two people looked into each other's eyes … well, it was very touching, to say the least. So much so that it would be enough to persuade the staunchest cynic to renew his or her belief in true love.

From that moment on, I was hooked by their energy and found myself unable to look away. Thank God they didn't notice me staring or surely would have had me kicked out of the place.

I spent the next several minutes thinking upon the love in my own life. With each passing thought, the reason behind this lakeside moment became clearer: I think this couple had been put in front of me as a simple reminder that love is all around me and, more than likely, is sitting right in front of me. A simple message, yet so profound.

I was grateful that I was able to receive evidence of divine presence through simple, everyday occurrences. I don't need to see the parting of the Red Sea in order to get it. In that particular moment, I was able to receive a message of love by merely sitting alongside a man-made lake.

Since those two lovebirds had inspired me so, I gathered the courage to walk over to their table and ask for their answer to my question.

Emil

> Pursuit! Regardless of misfortunes, or a world at odds with itself, there is a predominant factor that enables us to go forward and accomplish a measure of accomplishment toward happiness, liberty, and togetherness.

Ilene

> It seems to change somewhat as time goes on.... Family, friends, and a very good sense of humor.
>
> Sometimes you wonder why me and why am I here. I've watched my children grow, now my grandchildren. It's an extra plus when you have someone to enjoy all this with you, or a special *one* you love to be with.
>
> ... a lot more, but it would take twenty pages (a nice question).

... And from my favorite bartender at Waters ...

Armando

> The meaning of life to me is to wake up every morning and give thanks to God.

Work Pals

Once work pals, now lifelong friends …

So many of us think of work as a (bad) four-letter word. But befriending the following co-workers has helped me lengthen the four-letter-word list to include *love, hope, pure, give, kind, mend, open, true.* You get the picture.

I worked with Bobby, Gaynel, and Dee, circa 1977, at my first job out of college. As with most people in southern Louisiana, we worked in the "oil patch." When I met these three loving souls, I was a young, naïve, and timid southern girl. (No really, I was!) But after spending a lot of fun times with these hell-raising southerners … let's just say that I haven't been the same since, and I thank God for that.

I'm grateful when I have the opportunity to speak with them because of all the wonderful memories that come flooding back. Even though it has been over twenty-five years since I moved away from this trio, the love and admiration I felt for them so long ago continues to live in my heart today. One day, I hope I will be able to tell them just how much of an important role they played in my life, teaching me by their example how to be a true friend.

Until then, I remain grateful that we continue to share the desire to stay within one another's reach.

Bobby

I don't have a real deep or glamorous view of life. I see it as a journey, not unlike the path of a ball in a pinball machine. (I am obviously from the pre-video game era.) You are capable of tilting and ending the game, intentionally or not, at any moment. Those who tilt are cowards. You can choose to cling to the sides and avoid any contact. The penalty for this is a short and less-than-exciting trip. Or, you can take the path I chose—that is to try and hit every post, pillar, and springs along the way. A few have fatal results, but they are rare. Most of the obstacles only slow you down a bit. Some, you realize, you want to bump into often; still others send you back on your journey, opening opportunities for more contacts.

In all cases, you wind up in the same place. And that is exactly where you started. You're created by God and return to God.

Life is all about the path you take to get there and what you learn about the game along the way.

Gaynel

… an emotional roller-coaster ride where one's level of the soul moves toward the calmness of peace …

Dee

Love, joy, sorrow, friendships, family, disappointment. Without all these, life would not be complete.

◆   ◆   ◆

My relationship with Lindsey began in the mid-80s as a client/vendor association; I hired him to produce a training film for my company. We both have difficulty remembering the exact year we met, but what's the most important thing to me is that we have stayed close friends ever since, and my love and respect for him has grown with each year.

It is no easy task to describe Lindsey's complex nature and diverse lifestyle. Normally, I don't apply labels to people, but in Lindsey's case, it seems apropos.

Lindsey is a writer, film producer, scuba diver, pilot, adventurer, singer, explorer, loyal friend, humanist, confirmed bachelor, hiker, tennis player, voracious reader, boater, independent thinker, liberal, musician, loner and yet social …

Like the proverbial rolling stone, Lindsey "gathers no moss," so I look forward to adding more labels in the future.

Lindsey

> I think the meaning of life is something different for each living organism on the planet. We each have a unique place or role in the cosmos based upon where we happened to be born, the experiences we have, and the choices we make. We each determine the significance of what we do and who we are.
>
> Fundamentally, the meaning of life is to live. But some choose not to. Life is what each individual makes it. There is no right or wrong way to answer the question.
>
> I just hope people can give each other the acceptance and respect to make the determination on their own.

◆   ◆   ◆

I met Jeff around 1992 when I first started selling advertising space in the electronics industry. Jeff wanted to learn more about my publication because one of his clients was interested in doing business. So we scheduled our first meeting.

Now so far, this sounds like standard procedure in the sales world. However, I quickly learned that this was not going to be a typical sales call.

With directions to Jeff's office in hand, I hit the freeway heading to Los Angeles for our afternoon meeting. Jeff's office was located on the famed Hollywood Boulevard. After reaching the correct block, I parked my car, unloaded my gear, and began walking in search of his office building. Picture this: a Rebecca-of-Sunny-Brook-Farm-looking gal walking along Hollywood Boulevard wearing a business suit and toting a briefcase and a slide projector. Can you say "nerd"?

To say that I felt a little out of place would be an understatement. More accurately, I felt as if I was walking down the street with a neon arrow pointing the word "loser" at my head. And if memory serves, there were even a few people along my trek sitting in doorways, snickering as I walked past. But what the heck! Jeff was a hot lead, and nothing was going to stand in my way of making a sale.

After traipsing down Hollywood Boulevard for what seemed like an eternity, I eventually found Jeff's office building. I searched the front of the building for a sign. And there it was.

"No! This cannot be it!" I gasped aloud.

I checked my file to make sure that I had the right address, only to learn that I had arrived at the right place.

Again, I searched the front of the building for Jeff's sign, but there was only one: Frederick's of Hollywood.

That's right. My soon-to-be client shared offices with the famous lingerie store.

Trying desperately to keep the "Oh my God!" expression off of my face, I boldly entered the office with briefcase and slide projector in hand and asked to see Jeff. By now, the increased snickering that came my way was a moot point. I was just happy to no longer be wandering Hollywood Boulevard.

Of course, recounting my painful excursion only gave Jeff the biggest laugh of all. I won't even go into the details of having to show my slide presentation on the back of a T-shirt that was pinned to the wall. Had I known then that my meeting with Jeff that day was to be the start of a wonderful business relationship, I probably would have just hauled off and punched him and then joined in the laughter.

Jeff and I enjoyed doing business together for almost ten years, and even though a lot of time has since passed, I bet we still could laugh about our first meeting—with Jeff still laughing the hardest. But that is only fitting, because I will always remember Jeff for his big heart and even bigger ability to laugh at any situation.

Jeff

> It's the stuff that happens between one's plans for life.

◆   ◆   ◆

Throughout my career in the electronics industry, I had the privilege of working with the most talented and loving people, clients and co-workers alike. Like the saying goes, if some people leave a thumbprint on your heart, then I feel blessed to have my heart covered with the prints of these next people.

Mary

> The meaning of life—to experience joy, both giving and receiv-ing. To love others and nurture them. To revel in the magnifi-cence of nature. To find tolerance in our hearts and push ourselves to learn and grow. Life is the greatest gift, in all its forms. We are so blessed!

Scott

> Doing enough good to be remembered. Our lives are inter-twined, but to live life to its fullest one has to impact others, and I believe it is always best to do this in a positive way.
>
> We see people come and go all the time, but think about the people that have made an impact on your life. They will always be remembered; they are the ones that make us who we are. The

more positive people in this world, we will have a better rate for understanding survival. People are foundations of sorts for life. Each one is like a building block and helps us shape our thoughts.

I believe life on Earth is a glimpse of what is to come, but while we are here, we are actually building futures.

Beth

To me, the meaning of life is to ultimately find your soul mate. When you find your soul mate, you feel whole and complete. Until then, you always feel like a part of you is missing. You can make a lot of money, have a lot of things, enjoy your career, love your friends and family, and even have a good marriage and wonderful kids. But, when you find your true soul mate, it can bring all those things together and make everything more complete and enjoyable. There are so many things you can accomplish on your own, but with that special soul mate in your life, you are doubly strong.

So, I guess if I had to narrow my answer down to only one word, I would say "Love." A person can do without religion, government, laws, and even food for a short period of time. But without someone to love and love you back (whether that someone/soul mate is a friend, a lover, or whatever), then your life is ultimately unhappy and unfulfilled.

Nobody ever dies saying, "I wish I had a bigger house, or more money, or even more friends." Love is what makes the world go 'round, not money. Love ultimately leads to reproduction, and without reproduction, we wouldn't have people. We wouldn't have animals to feed those people, and we wouldn't have plants to feed those animals. They all reproduce.

Anne Marie

Making a difference and contributing. Being committed to others and helping them attain more meaning to their life. Being good to others and kind. Looking out for one another. Life is about being true to who you are and believing in yourself. And of most importance, being honest and being a friend.

At the end of the day, I'm true to my family, my friends, and my employer. I believe in being loyal to all and doing the best to represent each. You have to work at each, but the rewards and surprising happiness make it all memorable and meaningful.

Joy

What you believe in your heart and what you make of all that is presented and intersects with you.

Linda

It's interesting that such a complex question can sound so simple. To be honest, I have thought about this in some sense since I was a little girl. I remember sitting in my childhood bed, looking out the window at night, thinking about life and no life. Not death, but what if life didn't exist at all. It was a bizarre thing to ponder as a kid, and even as an adult. However, as an adult you have to ask yourself if you're fulfilling your own expectations of what your life should be. Which goes back to the original question—the meaning of life.

I think that it is different for everyone. I believe that we were given the gift of life to embrace as it best makes us happy. The meaning of my life is this: Make sure I'm happy the majority of the time. Make sure I contribute to other people's happiness (my friends, family, and kids). And make sure I leave the world better (or hopefully no worse) than when I got here.

What is the meaning of human kind? That's a whole other thought. Honestly, I don't know. I have different opinions at different points in my life. I do hope that we strengthen the world in terms of knowledge, compassion, empathy, and resources. I also hope that we learn to come together as a world with better understanding and patience for our differences. I don't believe that "life" as we know it will be threatened if we can't accomplish this.

Bill

It's who you are. Your family, friends, your experiences, your good times and your bad times. It's how others remember you long after you're gone.

◆   ◆   ◆

Cholas and I worked together at the same publishing company in the electronics industry for about thirteen years. From almost the first day I met Cholas, I knew he was a person who understood my personality, quirks and all. I think the reason behind Cholas's ability to quickly grasp the essence of a person is that he is a conscious listener, meaning that he not only takes in what is said by a person but also scrutinizes how it is said. Then, after listening without interrupting, he takes the time to ask great probing questions, clarifying any assumptions he may have made during the conversation. I loved that about him!

The day after I got "set free" from this job, Cholas strolled into my office to say good-bye.

"So, Weezie. What's your next move?" he asked.

"Well, I guess finding a job would be at the top of the list," I chuckled.

He listened while I tried on my thoughts of wanting to take some time off to regroup. After getting laid off, who has a clear mind of what they want to do on their last day of work? I was about to walk out of an office I had occupied for the last eleven years. How was I supposed to know where or when my next step would land?

True to form, Cholas listened intently, staring into me eyes to make sure I was telling him the truth. He weighed my words and then spoke.

"Weezie, let it come to you," he said.

His words immediately struck a chord in me and caused me to take stock of my life up to that point. I realized that I had always gone after the things that I thought I wanted or needed. Never had I let go of control and just allowed things to come to me. But for some unknown reason, the thought of "letting go," albeit a foreign concept to me, now felt good in my mind. I knew that I was going to spend a lot of time trying on his words.

Two years after that conversation, Cholas contacted me. It just so happened that his call came during a brief time when I had been toying with the idea of looking for one of those jobby things. Was his out-of-the-blue call a coincidence? I think not.

After a bit of catching up, Cholas admitted the real reason for the call.

"How about coming to work for me?" he asked.

The words had barely cleared his lips when I remembered his advice from two years before: "let it come to you."

The moment brought into focus the reality that for the past two years, I had actually practiced—hell, I all but perfected—the art of letting go of control to allow life to just happen, to unfold as it was meant to.

To this day, I begin each day with a commitment to let life come to me and to stand in awe and gratitude as I watch life work its magic.

Cholas

> Life is what it is meant to be. At the very least, it should be fulfilling. And when it isn't, you know. What you do to adjust the path to become fulfilled is the energy that life provides. It is not important to anyone else other than you. You may share it with others, but it should never be expected by others.

◆   ◆   ◆

Brenda was put on my path to teach me a few much-needed lessons—that of patience, acceptance, and tolerance. Since she hadn't volunteered to play the role of my teacher, I would venture to say that Brenda was unaware that I was learning many things from her during our time together. However, I would also guess that she was very aware of how miserably I failed at some of the lessons. Nevertheless, I continue to benefit from the knowledge gained, as I do from all the loving teachers who have graced my path.

When it comes to relationships, I'm the first one to admit that I set high standards for myself. I attribute this behavior to how I was raised by my parents. Looking back, I probably thought my parents were too strict or critical when a certain level of behavior was demanded from me. Now that I am much wiser—OK, much older—I have been shown the benefits of my upbringing many times over. For this, I truly am grateful to my parents.

It is not a big surprise (to anyone) that I'm guilty of holding others to the same high standards by which I was raised. Of course, this is unfair to do to someone, and I continually correct myself when I'm conscious of my actions. With some old programming still in place, I tend to desire things—people, places, and events—to be the way I want them to be, or more correctly, the way I was taught they *should* be.

It's because I acknowledge and accept the less-than-positive aspects of my humanness that I have developed a strong passion to become a better person. My passion has since grown into a strong "addiction"—one of self-growth. I admit to you now that I am a self-growth junkie.

Growth … good! Passion … good! Being a better person … good! Even though all of these things are good, I do admit that I tend to take it a bit further than most. When I'm experiencing the high from a "growth fix," I tend to drag along for the ride those people standing closest to me. Some very enlightened people volunteer for the ride.

Some come along out of curiosity. Others come along kicking and screaming criticisms of me the whole time. It is this last group of people that tends to get very annoyed with me, and of course, they have every right to feel that way.

My only recourse to the people I have annoyed in this manner is that I hope one day that they realize I loved them so much as to risk our relationship in order to build a foundation based on growth. Without growth, death is inevitable.

Brenda

> To live as God wants us to. We are only on this Earth for a very short time and need to live according to His word and commandments. Be patient, kind, and generous. Be loving, respectful of others, and slow to anger.

G'day Mates

It was on that Italian bus tour in 2001 I told you about earlier that I met married couples Ken and Glen and John and Rosalie. Both couples were native Australians but lived on opposite ends of the country. During the trip, these retired "kids" kept a watchful eye over me since I was traveling alone. How sweet is that? Their warm, generous spirits caused me to immediately fall in love with them.

One day, they asked if I would ever visit Australia. I answered by whining about the long flight and complaining that the standard two-week vacation that most Americans receive wasn't nearly enough to make the long trek worthwhile. I'm sure I tossed in a few more excuses but attempted to stop sounding like a pansy by assuring them that Australia was on my "gotta go there" list. Eventually, I weaseled out of the conversation by declaring the ever-optimistic sentiment, "Ya never know."

It was a year after first meeting my Australian mates that I was set free from my job. Now that I had some extra time on my hands, and a bit more willingness to endure long flights, I e-mailed my Australian mates and told them that I was finally ready to go "down under." Upon hearing the news, these wonderful people immediately offered to put me up for a week's stay in their houses, and on top of that, act as my personal tour guides. (You see how wonderful they are.)

I ended up staying in Australia for a total of three weeks—a week each in Sydney, Melbourne, and Perth. With each day, I fell more in love with Australia. It soon became apparent that spending even three weeks in the country was not nearly enough time to see all that it had to offer. It was, however, sufficient time for me to obtain confirmation that the entire county is filled with happy, easygoing people.

Over the years, my travels have afforded me opportunities to meet friendly people all around the world. Darlin', I was even born in a place known for its friendliness: the South. But I have found that there is something very special about Australians, though I cannot quite put my finger on it. It's not just that they are warm, open, and genuinely friendly. It's more like they possess an inner source of joy, of contentment, of something that I think is quite unique to their surroundings.

Through my "research" on these folks from down under, I found that Australians tend to foster a higher level of positive energy on a daily basis. Maybe it's because their daily conversations are filled with such customary sayings as "G'day, mate!" "Good on ya, mate!" "No worries!" These upbeat greetings may indeed be the only affirmation they need to be reminded that life is good. Sure, my research wasn't all that scientific, but if you don't believe me, go down under and see for yourself.

Many people have since asked whether I would ever go back. Let me just say that after only two days in the country, I began inquiring as to how I could get a work visa. Since I've been a walking advertisement for the country since my visit, I bet I could get a job working for the Australian Tourist Commission.

Bottom line: given the opportunity, I would return to Australia tomorrow on a one-way ticket!

John

A good partner. Love. Understanding. And lots of good health.

Rosalie

To live every moment of every day. But at the same time, take time out to appreciate the world around us.

Glen

> To me, the meaning of life is to bring a touch of heaven to the lives I meet as I journey on. What is heaven? It is faith, hope, and love. The greatest of these is love.

Ken

> Life is about love, relationships, and the way you share that love is the way you relate to those you meet, to those you respect, and wish to relate to. It's about choices you make and the way you live with those choices. It's about being happy with you as a person and contentment with that.

I feel so blessed that my "mates" were put on my path in life. Although it may be a while until we see each other again, I know that our hearts will always stay joined.

As I continued my "walk about", more wonderful Aussies crossed my path.

Yanni

> Happiness and being true to yourself.

Michael

> To be happy and satisfied and at peace with how I have lived up until this moment; and to be able to say the same when it's my turn to leave.

During the planning stage for my trip to Australia, I came across information on the Indian Pacific Railroad, a three-night train ride that cruises along an uninterrupted rail line from the Pacific Ocean in the east (Sydney) to the Indian Ocean in the west (Perth). The rail link, which crosses the treeless Nullarbor Plain, is famous for being the longest, straight stretch of railway track in the world (478 kilometers ... you do the conversion). The idea of taking such a unique trip appealed to me, and I booked passage straight away.

Sleeping on a train was a new experience for me. It was a hoot to be able to lie in bed and watch the landscape and wildlife of the Australian outback roll past my window. Although the entire train trip was very exciting, the true highlight of the trip was the good fortune of talking with my fellow passengers.

For some people, three days on a train may sound like a long time, but the unique experiences I collected from the trip made me wish that the train ride had been longer so that I could have collected more answers.

Kerri

> For me, life itself is the miracle, meaning that I don't really believe that anything happens once you die. Life is such an amazing gift, and the odds of you being formed and born are so long that the opportunity to have a life is the whole package, not the promise of an afterlife or reincarnation, or anything else.
>
> At times, I like to think of reincarnation, but if that's true, it's more than we should expect. Life is to be lived one day at a time. Always try to be in the moment and realize that nobody can affect you in any way unless you allow it.

Peter

> Forty-two would be my first answer.... Douglas Adams being behind that response. Sadly dead now, but so many people have asked this question and probably "42" is as meaningful an answer as any!
>
> "What is the meaning of life?" would be a tricky question, but as the question is currently worded, I consider life to mean all life. I might choose to answer scientifically or philosophically, but having a science background, I would probably try to explain the meaning of life in terms of the evolution of the universe. And I

would probably end with the conclusion/answer that life, as we know it is just complexity, and as such, has no meaning or purpose....

… and then there was Del. The story of meeting Del has become one of my favorites, ranking almost as high as the story of my Dad's passing.

I was the first to arrive at the dinner table, so I saved a seat for my newfound friend Kerri. As I looked out the window of the train and watched Melbourne slowly fade into the distance, a mature gentleman (Del) approached my dinner table and asked if he could join me. As I welcomed him to the table, I immediately took notice of his face, which seemed to be split in half. Although his mouth formed a smile, his eyes looked very sad, almost lifeless. I was deeply affected by this sight but chose not to let on to my impression. Instead, I continued with the conversation.

After a short exchange of pleasantries, I learned that Del was from northern California. *Gee, I come all the way to Australia just to be sitting across from a fellow Californian.* We shared a giggle over the lack of adventure in meeting someone from our home state. My giggling continued in hearing Del lament over the fact that when he was a younger man, he never had the courage to approach a woman as he had just done with me. Now that he was "no longer young," Del stated that women considered him to be "safe." Since Del was eighty-one years old, I admit that I shared that sentiment. Evidently, it seemed that the passing of time had taken care of Del's anxiety about approaching women.

As our conversation maintained a steady stream, I couldn't stop focusing on Del's face. The more I looked into his eyes, the more sadness I could see. I couldn't help but wonder what was causing him to be so sad. While focusing on his sadness, I heard Spirit's words.

Just listen to him.

I trusted and obeyed Spirit's direction.

After a bit more conversation, I asked Del why he was traveling alone. Sadly, he told me that Flo, his wife and best friend of fifty-six years, had passed away about six months earlier. I now understood the reason for his sadness. Del also shared with me that his own health wasn't the best and that this trip would probably be his last.

I was amazed at how much Del had shared with me in such a short period of time. It took me a while to digest it all. I couldn't relate to some aspects of Del's story, like being married for fifty-six years or losing my best friend. The only things that I could somewhat identify with was being alone and sharing a love of travel. I tried to imagine what it must feel like for Del to not only be suddenly alone in life, but also be forced to clip his own wings (stop traveling) due to illness. My heart grew heavy as I thought of the reality that Del now faced.

The next time I saw Del on the train, he contributed his answer for my book. To be quite honest, I didn't agree with Del's answer but through most of our discussion about it, I merely listened to him (as I was told to do by Spirit). I sensed that even though Del was mourning his wife, his answer hadn't come from a place of sadness or grief, but rather from his lifelong belief that there simply is no rhyme or reason to life. Del continued sharing his thoughts about his answer by admitting that neither he nor Flo believed in God nor had they ever followed a spiritual path of any kind. Instead, as an agnostic, he believed in a "rationalist philosophy." I believed quite differently and chose this time to speak up.

Knowing that Del and I were on opposite sides of this topic, I didn't want to alienate him by coming off as some aggressive, over-zealous preacher or worse. Instead, I shared with Del my thoughts and belief in God in the most gentle and loving manner that I could. He sat and politely listened, all the while probably wanting to shout out that he thought I was crazy.

My last comment to him was that I believed Flo was watching over him on this trip, and she also probably had a hand in our meeting. I also shared with him my mantra. Say it with me: *there are no accidents.*

It still makes me giggle when I imagine what Del must have been thinking of me at that point. Although he wore a poker face, I could see the wheels of thought turning in his head.

Del then began to tell his story of Flo's illness and recent passing, and he spoke about how his children were handling the loss. I listened to him for almost an hour. As our discussion came to an end, Del chuckled as he told me that his daughter (a therapist of sort) would have gotten a lot of money for what I had just done. Little did he know, I was being "paid" for my time in other ways.

The train pulled into Perth on Sunday. Everyone parted ways, without plans to see each other again.

My friends Ken and Glen met me at the train station, and from there, we began a wonderful weeklong sightseeing adventure in Perth.

Three days into my stay, Glen and I hopped onboard a ferry to Rottnest Island, where we spent the day on a bus touring the island. Our first stop at the west end of the island gave us time to stroll along the boardwalk, which snaked through a stretch of grassy dunes and ended at the water's edge.

As I made my way to the water, watching my every step so that I wouldn't fall off the boardwalk, I suddenly looked up and standing in front of me was Del. I could see by the look on his face that he was very surprised to see me. (Me ... not so much.) We hugged as if we were long-lost friends, all the while Del uttering his amazement of the "coincidence" of our seeing each other again. I merely responded with a knowing smile. *There are no accidents.*

I looked at Del and could immediately tell that something was different with him. This time when I looked into his face, not only was he smiling, but his eyes were also glowing and his entire energy was brilliant! Our short exchange didn't deliver a reason for his change in demeanor, but it was a welcome sight nonetheless.

My tour group was leaving, so I had to cut short our conversation. We said our good-byes. Del slowly turned away and then spun back toward me. With a twinkle in his eyes, he smiled, pointed his index finger up toward the sky, and nodded his head knowingly. His simple gesture spoke volumes.

In that moment, I knew that Del had, at the very least, opened his mind just enough to entertain the idea that someone "up there"—God or Flo—had something to do with our meeting … both times.

For me, Del was proof that when we let even a little Light into our heart and mind, our whole world becomes brighter.

I left Del that day feeling so very grateful that I had been able to connect with Spirit and receive God's message about Del: *just listen to him.*

Del and I continue to correspond. In one of his letters, written almost a year after our train meeting, Del wrote that he was becoming more and more amused with himself. He had to admit (especially to me) that he now found himself "loosening" his rationalist philosophy—a huge step for Del, and in the right direction, if I say so myself.

The moral of the story? For me, it was this: talk less and listen more with my heart. Blessings are indeed revealed in the silence.

Del

There isn't any. It's random events.

Cheerzini Pals

I think we've all wished at some point in our lives to have a *Cheers* type of place of our very own (just like in the sitcom), where we can walk in and be instantly greeted by friendly faces calling our name. Well, I'm very fortunate to have such a place—a wonderful restaurant in Irvine, California, called Vessia Ristorante.

When I first crawled into Vessia several years ago, I wasn't searching for a *Cheers* of my own. Actually, I was looking for a good restaurant with a relaxing atmosphere so that I could catch up on my reading and journal writing. Vessia fit the bill. The friendly atmosphere created by the ever-smiling servers, not to mention the wonderful food created by chef Gino, kept me coming back for more. However, my nights of quiet dinners ended the day I met one of Vessia's loyal regulars.

One night, instead of my usual two-hour dinner in the dining room, I decided to have a quick bite at the bar. I sat there for what seemed to be no more than a minute when the man next to me introduced himself as Bill. He was very friendly, and we exchanged the usual pleasantries, but it didn't stop there. As we chatted, Bill all too frequently stopped our conversation to introduce me to every single one of the regulars who walked into the restaurant. Good Lord, did he know everybody or what!

As more regulars streamed in, I became quite impressed by the friendliness and camaraderie of this Vessia community. Everyone displayed a genuine affinity toward the other through greetings of hugs and kisses. These regulars also greeted me, the newcomer, with such a degree of warm hospitality that it felt as if they were welcoming me to their own homes.

I soon learned that this colorful cast of characters regularly gathered for dinner at the bar, where they engaged in lively conversations and occasional heated debates ranging in topics from the sublime to the ridiculous. But no matter the topic, all were welcomed to toss in their own two cents.

Since that fateful night, I have become one of these regulars. Given the fact that I rarely have food in my house, I let Gino cook for me as often as possible. Along with the dubious honor of being a regular is the added privilege of passing along the hospitality once granted to me. Now when I see a stranger dining alongside me at the bar, I will introduce that person to all the regulars that I know. The beauty of this simple act is that after about five minutes, that person is no longer considered a stranger and will be warmly greeted the next time he or she walks through the door. If you think about it, don't we all just want to be known?

I guess if I had to name one downside to belonging to the Vessia community of regulars, it would be that my anonymity is a thing of the past. Those days of quiet dinners are long gone. But you know what? That's OK with me. As the *Cheers* song goes, "sometimes you want to go where everybody knows your name." I can only hope that at least a few of the Vessia regulars are glad that I came.

I've had several conversations with the people you are about to "meet," but it wasn't until they shared with me the stories behind their answers that I really had the opportunity to know them on a deeper level. Being entrusted with the details of their personal stories is by far the greatest gift I could receive.

Although I could write a story about most everyone from Vessia who contributed to my book, I'm singling out John. If memory serves, he was the first person who provided his answer for my book.

As I can already see John beginning to giggle as he reads this chapter, I must quickly confess that I rejected John's first two submissions. Hopefully, by the time you get to this page of the book, you will already have a sense of who I am and, therefore, be totally shocked to learn that I would ever reject a person's answer. (Well, I hope that's what you would feel!) Nevertheless, I did reject John's early answers. But before you start yelling at me for being so mean, let me explain the reason.

Over the years at Vessia, John and I have had the opportunity to delve into a few deep conversations. Through these conversations, it became apparent that John is not only a man of substance but also very loving and sensitive, especially when it comes to his daughters. The love that radiates from his eyes every time he speaks of his daughters truly touches my heart. Therefore, when I asked him to be a part of my book, I suggested that he think along the lines of writing words that he would leave to his daughters and future grandchildren. He liked that idea.

I read John's first entries, both quite brief in length.

"You're holding back," I scolded.

He could only laugh because he knew he was busted.

"You're writing this for your daughters, right?"

John replied cautiously, "Yes."

"Then as females, they're probably not going to be happy with a superficial answer. Right?"

"Yeah, you're right," he sighed.

"So then peel back a few layers and give them more detail, more meaning … more of *you* in your answer."

I climbed down from my soapbox and awaited his response. As harsh as it may have sounded, John immediately understood what I meant.

He lifted his head, held my gaze, and said, "Thank you. Thank you for the challenge."

Later on, I graciously accepted John's third entry.

With that, I give you John's words to his daughters….

Your life is a series of choices you make

A product of the paths you take

Each day a fresh start from beginning to end

A chance each time to begin again
We create the person we want to be
Our actions are our legacy

The manner that we choose each day
Defines our lives along the way
To take quick action or lag behind
Deciding if you'll give all you've got to give
Determines the life you elect to live

Then days, then weeks, then months, then years
Grow into a lifetime and soon it appears
That you've written the story that bears your name
The sum of your days and choices became
The book that is open for the world to see
Make sure it's the tale you want it to be

I am so proud of John for taking the time and effort to put his heart on paper for his daughters. I'm also very honored that he shared his words with me. His words serve as an inspiration to other parents to take the time to put pen to paper and craft their own loving message to their children.

No one was more surprised than I to turn around one day and see that these wonderful Vessia people, with whom I seemingly had nothing in common, actually had turned into great friends. What we have created within this neighborhood community of friends is very special. Fortunately, we know this and express our gratitude every time we meet.

Pauline

… to enjoy the company of wonderful friends. The pleasure of watching my grandchildren grow up. Watching the success of my three sons. The enjoyment of family time spent together. I guess the most special thing in my life if I think about it is my wonderful family and friends. The enjoyable time I spend with the love of my life, Bob.

Life is to be enjoyed to the fullest and I feel I do just that ... to the fullest. Life is what you make out of it. You get out of it what you put into it.

Bob

Spending time with a person you love and who loves you. Enjoying the accomplishments of your child. Developing camaraderie on the golf courses of the Earth with your friends. And having quiet time to enjoy all of the above.

Trisha

After an intensive, exhaustive work schedule, I know my joy, my life, comes from walking my dog. I get to notice the different hues of green in the bushes. I inhale the sweet, sweet scent of honeysuckle. I admire the bright pink of the "weeds," and marvel at nature that produces such hues. In this short forty-five minute experience, where I enjoy peace and contentment, I find meaning and revel in its simplicity.

Hugh

To prepare oneself for eternal life and make a contribution to the betterment of mankind whilst on this planet.

Alicia

Life is maturing to the point where one can make a difference. Choose when something isn't the best for us, learning to accept/ learn from mistakes and failures, and moving on when the time is right.

David

To create a journey for oneself along the way of which is discovery. The discovery leads to the answer. The connections we make make the meaning real. The loves we find give us meaning. The meaning of life is living a life filled with love, for that is all that endures.

"Lucy"

It's a very complex answer—too long to put into words. Life is the ups and downs of day-to-day tribulations, learning that we are not all either bad or good, but humans with goals and destinations that we are not always aware of until a certain time.

Life is learning from grief, happiness, failure, and success. Life is giving to others and not expecting. Life is living at the fullest and knowing every day is the best day of your life.

Owen

Procreation. Not only should we work at having children, but the world we leave them should be secure and sound and a better place than we were in. Improving, not diluting the quality of humanity.

Bill

Life is for the living.

Viki

If I answered this when I was twenty-one, I would have said independence—doing what I wanted to do, when I wanted to do it. If I had answered this at twenty-eight, I would have said having a family (children specifically). But now, I believe that it is family, and that family consists of people you meet along the way who can see who you are, love you through it, and that you can give back equally as much. And, to make that family bigger is the greatest gift that God can give you.

Rick

I think the question should be "What makes life worth living?" Life is a mixture of stimuli. Life is good when you are financially comfortable. Life is good when it is free of turmoil and bitterness. But truly what makes life worth living is when the sum of the parts is greater than the value of each individual. Nothing brings greater joy than when you enter a room and the intensity and joy of the people present raises because of your presence. The world is difficult. Trouble is around every corner. But when your addition to any event, conversation, or scenario increases the well-being of the participants, that is what it is all about. When you are present, people feel better about themselves and their lives; you have made an impact on someone's life in a positive way. Then, you can truly label yourself as a success.

Tom

To be able to, at any point along the way, truthfully claim to have pursued wisdom. And at the end of the journey, know you have done so in a veracious fashion.

Rick

Happiness. But most don't know what *happiness* means. It's not an euphoric state of well-being. It is simply "contentment with what happens." Notice the first four letters of *happy* and *happens*.

Jack

We don't know. We never will know until we die; and even then, we may not know. So, we focus on our purpose in life, our goals, our objectives, and our reason for doing whatever we do. I believe that we intuitively know what is good and what is evil. So our acts should be good and shouldn't be evil. If we do good, we should feel good. If we do evil, we should feel evil during life. If there is an afterlife, so much the better. If not, good is its own reward. Focus on the good in everything you do. I trust that if there is an afterlife, I will learn the meaning of my life. If I do good, that meaning I am sure will have been realized.

"Frany"

To always be an active player—passionate in expressing all true beliefs when requested or needed. Never to sit idle or passive. And expect things to grow prompted by listening to opportunities for change or growth.

Susanah

Who knows? At this stage in my life, given my age and life experience thus far, I would say happiness is key. I am thankful for every day and try to keep my life as simple as possible. Material possessions don't make me happy. Having people to love that give me love in return and lots of fun in the process give meaning to my life.

Jorge

Feel like you are alive.

"John"

I believe life is a series of experiences and relationships that the universe serves us so that we know why we were put here—or maybe so that in our next life, if we have one, we'll get to build on what we learned the first time around or the other times around (as many as there might have been so far). Or maybe all of the above is me just trying to sound wise.

Really, I think I'm just here for a while and doing the best I can and finally figuring out that I'm OK and that whatever I do or think or feel or say is OK as long as I'm not knowingly hurting anyone. And my job is to express "me" as much as possible.

Filippo

A number of years ago, I read a *New York Times* best seller by J. I. Packer entitled *Knowing God*. In the book, he stated that the chief end of man is to know God and to try to glorify him in every realm of life. In my life, this has caused me to rethink how I live my life and how I treat others. From an eternal standpoint, it has given me a hope regarding life hereafter. So the real meaning of life to me revolves around not just what I believe, but also in whom I believe.

Lynda

The meaning of life is to make a difference. Whatever your profession is in life, God put you here on Earth to make a difference in someone's life, if not a lot of lives. Also, I believe we are here to be happy, to enjoy the good, the bad, and the ugly, and to rise above it all and have fun. Party on …

Steve

It is the largest of all problems to answer…. Leave it to the attempts of science, philosophy, and theology to answer. I will wait until I hear God's complete truths. However, while I exist on Earth, I will continue to embrace its beauty, share it with compassion, and aspire for transition.

Celebrate life!

Dhale

Life is the opportunity to become a part of someone's memory.

Mary

The meaning of life to me is having a goal of living the best life I can. That is, to be kind, thoughtful, respectful, and to give people the benefit of the doubt that they are good, honest people.

It is also finding someone that I can give my life to completely, to share happiness, sad times and challenges with, and to know that the person will still love me unconditionally, just as long as I am honest with him.

The meaning of life to me has nothing to do with material things but has everything to do with how I live my life, how I can impact others in a good way, and the good works that I do for others.

Eric

I have no idea what the meaning of life is. All you can do is live life the best you can, and when you die, only then will you find out what is the meaning of life.

Arend

To do on Earth what you're earmarked to do. Making a difference in the lives of other people and fulfilling your true potential. Following the guidelines as prescribed in the Word will help you achieve that.

Don

I will take the liberty of defining *meaning* as "purpose." I'm sure it is, at least, a synonym. Therefore, the purpose of life is to live it in such a way as to have no regrets. Seek to accomplish much. Travel. Explore. Invest. Experience much!

Treat others with respect. Help those in need. Be kind, compassionate, and benevolent. Live honestly, with character and integrity.

And through all this hopefully influence others to do the same…. Yes, to live life with no regrets!

Peter

The meaning of life is to experience everything God puts on our path, and to take those experiences and pass on what we learned from those experiences. Sharing and loving all!

Lisa Jimenez, M.Ed.—best-selling author of *Conquer Fear!*

Mmmm ... To me the meaning of life is to be love. Another way to say this is to manifest God! This is exciting to me because I can see a planet where all people are in unity with God and with each other. Love is the most powerful force on the planet. It heals. It creates. It manifests ... and it brings out the best in every person.

I've learned that if I want to love, I choose to strip myself of all labels and trust that just showing up and *being* is enough. When I am willing to release all "labels," trust in the Living, Loving God, and show up fully, I will be a vessel to give love and receive love. Wow! This must be what Jesus promised when He said, "I am preparing a place for you ... that's beyond what you can think or even imagine." Amen.

OK, I confess. I allowed this next answer (from Craig) to be e-mailed to me. But since he is a judge, I thought that I might have to call in a favor one day.

Craig

My first thoughts were two ... to find fulfillment and truth. There are more aspects I'm sure, but I'm sticking with my first two thoughts.

Fulfillment. What satisfies ... even temporarily, the sense that I exist for something than myself? Is that self-centered? That answer probably depends on one's motivation ... but for some people, definitely yes. To steal from the concept of "paying one-self forward," is it good deeds I've done in favor of my fellow man? Accomplishments of all varieties? My "mark" or legacy? All of those and probably more, I'm sure.

If I take an extra two to three minutes in my workday to talk to a young man or woman about the dangers inherent in drinking and driving … or drug use … it probably doesn't matter to most of them. If even one is "turned around," I probably won't know it. My hope is that they will change, and the prospect that if even one of them hears me, and does change, it will be worth the time.

I have two children. Parenting them is fulfilling to me. I've done it solo for a long time. As my son left home last night I followed him out to the driveway. He hugged me and said, "I love you, father" … and I know that he does. My daughter is in Oregon for a week and calls me at night to talk. She wants to tell me about her day and find out what I've been doing … she talks with her brother. These children of mine are good, caring people that will live after I'm gone.

Truth … how did I get here? Why am I here? How should I live my life? Then what? As I get older, truth looms for me as one of the bigger questions in my life. It seems I know a lot of people who have died … in my opinion, prematurely. Children. My younger brother. Friends. I am still saddened by their deaths.

Truth for some people is in acquiring things. Money … or their work. Religion provides many people with "truth" about life's important questions. I think that parenthood, more than any single event, has opened my eyes to the value of religion and the role it should play in my life. The unconditional love that I have as a father, for my children, is instructive of God's love for each of us. I don't believe this is just an accident of evolution. My belief and my faith in God have had a growing influence on the choices I make in life. I continue to grow and evolve in my understanding, and by the time I die, I suppose I still won't have it all figured out.

Larry

Personally, happiness, and fulfillment through doing for others, leaving the Earth and everything in and on it better off for me being here.

If We Never Meet Again

My friendship with Kimberly started in 1995 and lasted for about eight years. Somewhere during the midpoint of our relationship, I "adopted" her as my sister—not something I do lightly because I consider sisterhood to be sacred. However, I think we both realized from the start that our relationship was going to be challenged by the fact that we had very little in common. Despite that fact, I still did my best to keep our relationship going. You see it was during this time that I was trying to recreate the bond that I shared with my sisters. Perhaps another reason the relationship lasted was that we thought that it *should* survive because it had such potential. Is that not a female's way of thinking or what?

As our lives continued to move in opposite directions, Kimberly and I spent less time together, and as a result, less time nurturing our relationship. In the end, the relationship ended.

When I think back on our friendship, I am always reminded of a piece of advice offered to me long ago: *Relationships are like flowers. It takes a little water every day to keep them alive.* As with flowers, the relationships that are important to us need to be tended to and nurtured on a regular basis.

But as they say, things change and life goes on.

Kimberly

> The meaning of my life on Earth is to leave this place better for having lived.

For me as a mother: to teach my children morals and values; to give them security and open mindedness as a way of life; to share love passionately; to share thoughts intimately; to be faithful.

As a friend: to be supportive and celebrate joy and success and to offer support in times of need.

As a person: to be forgiving, embrace differences, and do the unexpected act of kindness.

But life doesn't end when the body ceases to exist … it's just the beginning of a deeper, spiritual life that we can only imagine.

There are always people that come into your life without fanfare but make a lasting mark nonetheless. I just had to capture the answers from a few of these lovely folks.

Georges

So … you want to know my opinion of "the meaning of life." That very thought conjures up images ranging from the humorous talk-show host to the meditating Buddhist monk. But, then again, you asked for mine, not theirs.

My meaning of life is to experience as much happiness as possible. Does that answer then beg the question, "What is happiness?" If yes, then let's start by defining what it is not. It is not: having fun, satiating the senses, self-indulgence, excelling, accumulation of things, or receiving from someone. Happiness does not come from the outside. It comes from the inside. It is that state of being in which one mentally knows and emotionally feels that his or her decisions and subsequent actions have been made for the purest of motives, that is, mindfulness. Happiness is the consequence of mindfulness.

The meaning for my life is reached by being as mindful as possible. Achieving that is a constant struggle, which brings me to my dilemma—is it the struggle to achieve happiness or the happiness that is the meaning of life …?

Rae

My first response is, "meaning, there is no meaning to/of life."
My second response wanted to be a monologue on my life history
of trials and tribulations. But there is a third idea lurking in the
recesses of my head. I'll see if I can verbalize these ideas and write
them down.

I sit here waiting for ideas to gel, to become words on paper,
to become symbols of my mind, and I find—nothing. No words,
no symbols, no cute phrases, trite remarks, no quotable quotes.
Emptiness; a quietness; an absence of words in my mind. Just a
soft hum. Thoughts are flitting through my mind, with no connection to anything. What is going on? Why is it becoming so
difficult?

As I am trying to figure out what to write, the answer suddenly appears. The meaning of life … learning about the absence
of words, letting go of the need to use words, to describe Spirit.
Finding Spirit is the meaning of life or the reason for life.

Finding Spirit within (with no words) is the only thing that
matters in life. When you find Spirit, you will have all the
answers.

Emelia

Being happy doing everything you want to do. Enjoying the people you love and spending time with them, because when you die,
the memory of how you lived will stay with the people that knew
you.

Susan

Being of a spiritual nature, I feel that we are all here for a purpose.
What that is, only God knows. But we must do our best to follow
our beliefs to make sure that our existence is worthwhile and that
we don't mess up too much.

Kristen

> What gives life meaning is the meaning of life. For me, it is the love, generosity of oneself, your heart and soul that is shared. It may be in a long-lasting friendship or a relationship with family that is nurtured over time or kindness given to someone you barely know when they cannot take any more of what life has to give. Being there for someone in whatever forms that may take.

Wendy

> Life, to me, is the opportunity to put into practice all the lessons learned, to "untwist the world" for others, sharing what knowledge one has gained so far. To put oneself in situations where learning and growing can occur and be shared, and to love and appreciate every opportunity to make a difference.
>
> To me, life is all about listening to the universe and acting in response, always with the goal of making each moment a more positive one than the last.

◆   ◆   ◆

I met John in 1996 while partying in the "hood" (my slang for the neighborhood of Corona del Mar). But to put our relationship on higher ground, John was also a member of my church. In the beginning of our relationship, I saw John in church every Sunday, which is apropos since I am about to tell you my "Church Story."

Throughout the time I knew John, his dad had been quite ill, battling several serious ailments over the years. John would (lovingly) joke about his dad's ailments, saying that any one of them alone should have "done him in" a long time ago. But joking aside, I could see that John was proud of his dad for being such a relentless fighter. With my own dad passing the year before I met John, I could understand a bit of what John was going through and my heart went out to him.

Shortly after hearing about the illness of John's dad, I wasn't surprised when I received a message (I believe from Daddy): *always be there for him because you know what it's like.*

Since I never had the courage to argue with Daddy when he was alive, I certainly wasn't going to argue with him now that he was on the other side.

After about a year of knowing John, our contact stopped. Even though we would run into each other a few more times around town, several years passed where I didn't see him. But out of the blue one day, I received a message from Spirit.

Go to church!

Now, admittedly, I had stopped going to church a couple of years prior. (I don't believe spirituality is exclusively tied to organized religion.) So I did my best to ignore the message. However, ignoring this particular message was about as easy as ignoring that proverbial elephant in the room. The message just kept repeating over and over.

Go to church! Go to church! Go to church!

All right, already!

I sat in church that following Sunday, wondering why I had been called there. All the obvious reasons came to mind, like maybe Momma had found out that I had stopped going to church and put out a celestial APB for my church arrest. Or maybe she had her prayer circle chant loud enough for me to hear it hundreds of miles away. Or my favorite, maybe I had been called to church to meet my next boyfriend. Well, long story short, none of these guesses were even close. (Bummer about the last one.)

As the mass continued, it reached the part of the service when a prayer is said for the sick and dying and the names of the recently departed are read aloud. John's dad was on the list.

I felt numb at hearing his name. I began to cry at the thought of the pain John was now going through and would endure for a long time to come.

In that moment, the reason why I had been called to church that day had been revealed. I knew without a doubt that Spirit had sent me to church so that I could learn of the passing of John's dad.

It did my heart good to link Daddy's initial message to me—*Be there for him*—with that of Spirit's. I think Daddy's message ultimately helped me stay open to receiving the message about going to church and, hence, hearing about John's dad.

For me, it made for a perfect "full circle" moment.

John

> A question without a single answer. Indeed, were there an answer, we need not take the journey. I suppose, to me, the answer changes/evolves as I proceed through life.
>
> As a young man, I felt it was important to do well and succeed. As I have grown older, gotten married, and had a child, my perspective has changed. I have always known that a relationship with God and family was important. However, as a parent, I now *believe* it.
>
> I believe living life in a way that you set a good example for your children and raising good children is the meaning of life in the truest form. There are lots of other goals and meanings of life, but I believe the children I raise and leave behind for the world is how I ought to be judged and the most important thing I will do in my life.

◆   ◆   ◆

My hairstylist Torey and I shared a giggle every time we spoke about the first day we met, circa 1999. I made an appointment with Torey based on the recommendations of several ladies in my office. Since I wanted to make a drastic change to my hair, I decided to push the envelope and have someone new cut it.

As with most stylists, Torey began the appointment with a consultation, during which time I told him that I wanted my hair cut short.

Really short. I even pointed to pictures to give him an idea of just how short I wanted it. Upon hearing my request, Torey got this strange look on his face, finally admitting that he was a bit nervous to make such a drastic change since this was his first time with my hair.

Eventually, I convinced Torey that I wouldn't beat him up over a haircut. *It's just hair!* So after a few deep breaths, both scissors and hair started flying.

Torey and I have giggled many times about how nervous he was that day, and I continue giggling when I think back to the look on his face.

I enjoyed the wonderful friendship Torey and I developed through the years. Granted, our relationship developed over one-hour increments every two months, but even in those short spurts of time, we were able to share our deep love for God and family.

Oh, about that first haircut … yes, he cut it short. Really short.

Torey

> Relationships. I am a hairstylist and have been blessed with a life of interacting with so many different kinds of people. I believe the dear Lord has created us to build relationships. We learn from every person we meet, each child we have, and we grow from everyone. Without relationships, what would life be?

◆   ◆   ◆

Nagisa (which means "broad shore") has been a thriving sushi restaurant in Corona del Mar, California, since 1982, and I have been a loyal customer for over a decade. However, I have confessed to owner Ray that I do sometimes cheat on him by going elsewhere for my sushi fix.

Even though several good sushi restaurants are a stone's throw from my house, I stick with Nagisa because it's quite special. Maybe it's the fun atmosphere created by the friendly diners at the sushi bar.

Or maybe it's the high-quality fish prepared by the skilled knife of head chef Yasu. But if I had to name one reason that makes Nagisa special, it would have to be Ray's charm.

Ray

Enjoying. Richness. Good living.

A Slice of a Dream

In choosing from a rather lengthy list, one of my favorite local places to vacation is Catalina Island. Catalina is located about twenty-two miles from Los Angeles and has a year-round population of about 3,500.

To reach this Pacific island paradise, Southern Californians (and tourists alike) either hop on board smooth-riding catamarans for an hour-and-a-half boat ride or take a fifteen-minute helicopter ride. Mainlanders in particular use the island as their private retreat to get away from the stress of everyday living in a megalopolis.

Once on Catalina, it's quite refreshing to experience the island's version of a traffic jam—two or three golf carts arriving simultaneously at an intersection. Since very few cars are permitted on the island, residents and visitors are limited to a few modes of transportation: golf cart, scooter, bicycle, or on foot. This is hardly an inconvenience, as Avalon—the only city on the island—is about one mile long, making for short distances between any two points of travel.

Avalon is nestled between a tranquil backdrop of rolling hills and the crescent-shaped harbor, which is always dotted with beautiful yachts and sailboats. High above the town rests my favorite place to stay on the island: the Inn on Mt. Ada. I call it my mansion. (One can dream!) The Inn, better known as being a past residence of chewing gum mogul William Wrigley Jr., sits high atop Mt. Ada, which is named for his wife.

Sitting on the Inn's front veranda allows you to gaze dreamily across uninterrupted miles of azure blue water. Occasionally, your peaceful trance is interrupted by the sound of a bird's graceful wings swooping past on a gust of breeze as it heads to the nearby hillside looking for its next meal. To the rear of the property are rolling hills, alive with wildflowers and native wildlife, stretching as far as the eye can see. No matter the direction of your gaze, the beauty that surrounds the Inn is sure to soften your soul to a state of bliss.

With each visit to the Inn, I've noticed that it takes only a few minutes of being on the property before I begin devising a way to either extend my stay or make a return trip as soon as possible. In addition to the Inn's beauty and picturesque island setting—both equally worthy of the trip—another draw of my stay there is the way I'm treated, like a part of the family. This is artfully accomplished through the gracious hospitality of innkeepers Susie and Marlene, along with their pampering staff, who go out of their way to create a wonderfully relaxing environment.

The list of good things I could say about my experiences at the Inn on Mt. Ada would stretch a mile. Come to think of it, I guess I shouldn't speak so highly of the place in the event that I won't be able to get a reservation next time! But no matter. It does my heart good to let people know of a place where they can live a slice of a dream.

Susie

> The meaning of life is love. The question at the end of life will be "How well did you love?" The lesson to learn in this lifetime is how to love—everything (people, animals, thoughts, food, knowledge … ourselves).

Gifts from Above

Flying is one of those events in life that motivate most people to pray—for a safe landing or for their luggage to land at the intended destination.

Before my return flight from my friend's Hawaiian wedding, I also said a pseudo prayer before boarding the plane.

God, please let me sit next to the cute guy on the plane ... and make sure he's single!

I do believe that God has a sense of humor and forgives me for taking up his time. But really, is it too much to ask to sit next to a guy who could make me yell "yeehaa!" for the duration of my five-hour flight home?

After my brief chat with God, I boarded the plane and waited to meet a special guy.

A few minutes later, "Harry" came onboard and was escorted to the seat next to me. Yes, he was a total cutie and he was single, but he seemed quite shy and kept to himself during the early stages of the flight. Incidentally, I should note that whenever I fly, I always give space to those sitting around me because I appreciate the same in return. However, when I noticed Harry having difficulty opening his bag of peanuts, my heart wouldn't allow me to just sit there and do nothing. I mean, I couldn't let him starve! So, I broke the ice by offering my assistance.

"Hold on," you might say. Why did this shy cutie pie need help opening his bag of peanuts? Well, as I was soon to learn, my seatmate was a sneeze away from turning ninety-one years old! Yeah, yeah, I know; this certainly was a case of being careful what you wish for.

After introductions were made, Harry and I passed the time by talking about many things. The first words he spoke that rang true to me were, "Kids today move too fast." Since I had just spent a relaxing week in Hawaii, I was quick to jump on the people-move-too-fast bandwagon. Oddly enough, that's all it took for us to launch into deeper and more personal topics.

I politely peppered Harry with many questions, and he freely answered them all.

"What brought you to Hawaii?" I asked.

"Oh, my daughter thought the family needed a getaway," he replied. Then he continued in a whisper, "My wife just passed away two months ago."

"I'm so sorry."

"We were married for sixty-three years," he added.

In the back of my mind, I started wondering what it would be like to be married to someone for sixty-three years. I will never know what that is like. Frankly, I'm hard-pressed to remember the last time that I dated someone for sixty-three days. (Unfortunately, I'm not kidding.) So being with someone for sixty-three years is well beyond my comprehension ... but enough about my pathetic love life.

I tiptoed into my next question.

"So, what's the secret to having such a lasting marriage?"

"I don't know," he chuckled, "but when you have a good wife and good kids ..." His words trailed off, leaving him with a contented smile on his face.

Our conversation continued for well over an hour, but as we both were in need of a nap, I asked a final question. "What is it like to grow old?"

He thought for a moment and then replied, "You cry. You cry alone."

"Harry"

> First of all, what is the meaning of life? It's a big question mark.
> And, actually, if you want to know the truth, I really don't see all
> the answers. Tomorrow is a new day, and everybody should be
> happy. You wake up in the morning ... it's OK. If you don't, you
> don't have to worry about it. Life is about the time being. Life is
> short and sweet. Life is sweet. If children come into this world as
> good, they'll be good. If not, you do your best. It's not easy. It's
> not easy.

Based on my experiences traveling with Momma, I highly recommend that everyone, no matter your age, take a trip with an elderly person or two. I've found that traveling with or even alongside a person (as with Harry) of wiser years is so very rewarding. For me, experiencing the world through their eyes adds value and meaning to the philosophy "stop and smell the roses."

By listening with my heart, I continue to learn from the elders of our "tribe." Slow down ... breathe deeply ... and look at life through grateful eyes.

A few months later, on yet another flight, I encountered a "flying angel." Our meeting took place on the flight home from Momma's house after her stroke. Little did this angel know, but her simple touch helped heal my wounds.

After Momma's stroke, I spent three weeks acting as her private Nurse Ratched. For the first time in my life, I was the one in charge of Momma's well-being instead of it being the other way around. Well, OK maybe not in charge per se, but I helped where I could, from checking that she adhered to her doctor's instructions to helping her move about the house so as to make sure she didn't fall.

I must admit that I had some fun during my nursing gig. I really enjoyed cracking the whip whenever Momma tried to weasel out of doing her physical therapy exercises, and I also had fun taking away her walker when it became too much of a crutch. It wasn't like I was on a power trip or anything. No, really! And I totally disagreed with those who thought my tough love approach was my way of getting even for my childhood. Can you say "payback"?

But seriously, I was so grateful to be able to spend time with Momma at such a critical point in her life. However, the fun went away when I realized that she and I were experiencing role reversal, that inevitable yet dreaded stage of life shared between a parent and a child. I always knew it was going to happen some day, but I guess it had started sooner than I expected.

The stroke left Momma in such a helpless and vulnerable condition, which was extremely hard to accept at first. Outside of the occasional cold or flu, Momma had never been ill in her life. But oddly enough, after the initial shock wore off, her condition ceased to upset me. Instead of feeling sad or depressed about Momma, my attitude stayed positive, which gave me the strength to quickly accept the situation and do what had to be done to get her better.

I also think keeping a positive attitude may have kept me from crying during the entire three weeks that I spent with Momma. Nope, not once did I cry—which is quite a feat for someone who cries over TV commercials. Instead, I remained strong … until my flight back home.

Once the flight took off, I began processing everything that had happened during my stay. I pictured Momma's face crying as she begged for her life to return to normal. Her spirit was crushed by the first blow of old age. Uncertainty and fear hung over her head when she thought of what lay ahead. Was this the beginning of the end?

I allowed the weight of the situation to sit on my heart. Since I was in a place where I didn't have to put up a good front, I gave myself permission to feel all of the emotions that I had smothered for the past few weeks. Suddenly, the tears burst forth and flowed in a constant stream as if they were trying to wash away my face.

A napkin was all that I could hide behind to keep the world from knowing that I was crying like a baby. So much emotion rose up, but I didn't try to control it. I chose to just let it all flow freely.

God (and those around me) only knows how loudly I wailed, when from my left side, I felt a hand gently rest on my shoulder.

"Are you OK?" asked Stacey, a sweet-eyed woman who had not been in her thirties for very long.

Even though I was an emotional wreck and had wet stuff pouring out every possible hole in my face, it made me laugh to think that my first thought was to say, "Yes, I'm OK." But I looked at her through my tears and shook my head. "No."

Admitting the truth made even more tears flow.

Once my sobbing subsided (and all of the runny stuff had been wiped from my face), we began to talk. I learned that she was also returning from a long stay playing nursemaid to her mother-in-law, who was recovering from a recent surgery. *There are no accidents in life.* We both got a big kick out of comparing notes on recovering mothers!

Our conversation eased my mind and allowed me to regain my composure and sit quietly for the duration of the flight. I'm sure my silence was a welcome change for the people sitting around me.

In my mind, Stacy was an angel for opening her heart and reaching out to a stranger in need. She was a perfect example of humans at our best. No matter our flaws and shortcomings, the human spirit comes alive at the perfect time.

For her loving efforts (and success) in comforting this weepy traveler, I will always remember Stacy and will be forever grateful for her compassionate spirit.

Stacy

> Across all religions, a basic tenant prevails: treat others as you wish to be treated. Call it karma, the golden rule, call it anything you want—just do it.

The meaning of life is to get through it as easily, happily, and above all, as peacefully as possible. And the only way to fulfill this meaning is to follow the golden rule.

Canyon Bliss

I didn't receive any money for saying nice things in this book about the places to which I have traveled (bummer!). Therefore, when I do recommend a travel spot, there are no outside influences swaying my words. I choose to speak of places with which I have felt an internal connection, places that have touched my heart and soul.

This is exactly what happened in the summer of 2003 when I hopped in a rental car and traveled the famed Loop Tour of the southwest.

I learned about the Loop Tour from a wonderful PBS program. In the early 1920s, the Union Pacific railroad created the Loop Tour to help encourage tourism in the southwest. In addition to the efforts of the railroad, the "loop of lodges" was created in southern Utah so that tourists could easily be connected to all three of the states' national park treasures—Zion Canyon, Bryce Canyon, and the Grand Canyon North Rim—and their respective lodges.

Here is a bit of trivia: even though the entire Grand Canyon National Park rests in northern Arizona, the North Rim was included in the loop because it's only a short drive from Kanab, "Utah's Gateway to the Grand Canyon National Park."

Intrigued by the story of the loop, I immediately jumped online to book accommodations at all three national park lodges.

When I think upon my canyon trip, I'm reminded of the saying "life is about the journey, not the destination." For this particular trip, I enjoyed the best of both worlds, as the journey and the destination were equally magnificent.

With every click of the car's odometer, breathtaking views of nature paraded before my eyes. Deer grazed in meadows. Wildflowers edged the roadside. Violent thunder and lightning storms rolled across the purple horizon. OK, I could have done without the scary lightning storm, but I think you get the picture. The time I spent driving to each of the canyons was filled with indescribable beauty.

As for the beauty of the canyons themselves, how can I describe them without writing volumes? From the pink rock pinnacles ("hoodoos") of Bryce Canyon to the deep, narrow canyons and immense rock formations of Zion to the spectacular color and sheer grandeur of the Grand Canyon, it can all be summed up in three words: ya gotta go!

Long before setting out on this journey to "God's country," I knew I had to talk to people who had left the chaotic rat race to establish a life in the serenity of nature's embrace. In my opinion, it takes an exceptionally evolved and courageous person to shift gears in life and change his or her lifestyle. Such people would definitely stand out in the crowd, and I just had to talk to them.

I'm not sure whether it was the twinkle in their eyes or the calm, relaxed demeanor that gave them away, but these "canyon people" (as I call them) seemed to have a joyous spirit and peaceful aura that echoed *We have it good here!* And their answers confirm that sentiment.

JR

Doing what makes you feel great.

Mike

I believe that life is meant to be enjoyed to the fullest. For one to explore the land and meet as many people as possible. To not be tied down to one place and not to revolve around the almighty dollar. That is merely my opinion.

Bethany

For me, it is to gain as much intellectual knowledge as possible. And then to combine, sift, and finally create a sort of dish out of the blending of book knowledge, actual physical experience, metaphysical enlightenment, accomplishments—most importantly mistakes—and finally encounters and emotions. When the dish is finished—and it never really is—then I'll know the meaning of my life.

Bill

To love lots.
To have fun.
To help others.
To enjoy every day.

Ken

Being able to live life to its fullest and enjoying the people you are surrounded by.

Connie

Life is love for all, no matter how good or bad. Life will go on.

Shawn

I feel the meaning of life is to enjoy each day to the fullest. Be happy and smile, and it is contagious. God only gives you so many days on Earth, so you better enjoy them.

Marty's Story

Thursday, November 13, 2003—the one-year anniversary of when I started writing my book. If you recall from the first chapter, I actually started writing my book on the night of my birthday. So now that you know my birthday, I expect presents from now on.

To mark this dual celebration, it was only fitting that I make a pilgrimage of sorts to where it all began: Bayside Restaurant. When I arrived at the bar, oddly enough, the only chair that was available happened to be just one chair away from where I sat one year before. And what do we think about "accidents" in life? Of course, I saw this as a sign.

Although I was understandably charged with excitement on this special night, I also sensed that something was about to happen ... something very special. With the support of my usual "bring it on" attitude, I was open to all the possibilities that were meant to happen in that particular moment in time.

The night had a slight chill in the air, but the restaurant was quite warm and cozy. Its dimmed lights cast a romantic haze across the room. Oh, why do I choose such romantic settings when I am alone? Maybe it's because I'm not afraid of them.

After ordering my drink, I nestled into my chair and decided to focus all of my excitement into writing a much overdue letter to my train friend Del. I was making great headway on it when the man sitting to my right broke my concentration.

The man made a simple comment, a play on words over the name of the wine I had ordered. I politely acknowledged his comment and returned to my writing. A few minutes later, he tossed more comments my way, something about the commercial on TV. Before I responded this time, I quickly glanced at his ring finger (old habit) and noticed a wedding band. Not only was he wearing a wedding ring, but come to find out, his wife was sitting right next to him. Yikes!

I must confess that I initially thought it a bit odd for a married man to strike up a conversation with a woman while in the company of his wife. However, Spirit quickly corrected my mind and told me that he was merely trying to be friendly. Nevertheless, out of respect for his wife, I made sure my replies were polite but brief. However, a few seconds later (you guessed it), he volleyed yet another comment my way.

Noticing that I was writing in my journal, he asked, "Doing some work?"

I just had to giggle with delight at his remark because it reminded me of meeting Carlos one year ago this night. At this very restaurant. Sitting in (almost) the same chair. And Carlos had asked me the same question. As you know, Carlos ended up being the first entry in my book. Were the planets aligning, or what?

"No, it's not work," I said with a smirk, knowing that something was in the air.

With this kind of synergy working in my favor, I knew I had to surrender to the moment and converse with this man. God knows he had worked hard enough for it.

The man and I—and his wife, thank you very much—immediately launched into a wonderful conversation about how fun it is to meet people along life's path. Then, in a flash, the man changed the subject and began speaking of his four-year-old son, Alex. And then as suddenly as before, the man left (for the bathroom, I presumed).

As he left, he remarked to his wife, "Tell her the story of Marty."

Who was Marty?

The man's wife, who may have been as amazed by the energy of the moment as I, began telling me the story. I only had to hear a few words to know that I was about to hear something personal.

I interrupted her story and said, "My name is Louise." I extended my hand.

She returned the handshake with a giggle, acknowledging the fact that the whole time we were laying the groundwork for an exchange to occur, not one of us had thought to introduce ourselves.

For the record, I had been talking to Brian and Susan all this time. Marty (short for Mardelle, a name given to her by French nuns) was Brian's sister.

After the introductions, Susan then picked up where she had left off.

"At forty-nine years old, Marty was diagnosed with cancer," Susan said. "And soon after the diagnosis, she was hospitalized. Something amazing happened during one of my visits with her at the hospital."

Susan took a deep breath, "We were talking, and then all of a sudden she looked at me and said, 'Congratulations! You will be so happy.' Well, I didn't have a clue as to what Marty was talking about but I didn't ask her about it.

"A few days after the visit," Susan continued, now with a puzzled look on her face, "I had this funny feeling that came over me. Just a 'certain feeling.' I eventually gave in to the feeling and took a pregnancy test. The test came out positive. I was pregnant.

"As soon as I saw the positive test result, I instantly knew what Marty had meant by her offer of congratulations. Somehow Marty had known that I was pregnant."

Susan's mood became somber. "The next day, just one day after I learned that I was pregnant, Marty died."

One spirit leaves, another enters.

At this point in the conversation, Brian jumped back in and picked up where he had left off talking about his four-year-old son, Alex.

"Personality plus," Brian said, with Susan nodding in agreement. "Everyone who meets Alex says the same thing: 'he could be the mayor today.'" As with most proud parents, Brian and Susan were sure that some day Alex would make a positive impact on the world.

Brian enumerated the endless list of similarities shared by his sister and Alex, supporting the couple's profound belief that Marty's energy and spirit was alive and well in their son. "I can see signs of Marty in Alex's eyes and in his smile," he said. "Alex even has Marty's signature laugh."

I felt so honored that Brian and Susan had chosen to share their story with me and so moved by it that I just couldn't hold back from asking them to be a part of my book.

I launched into the explanation of how I ask everyone to answer the same question, but before I could finish, Brian interrupted. "Is the question like *what is the meaning of life?*"

Just so you know, I didn't have anything lying around me that would have given away the question. Absolutely nothing! But considering the fact that so many events that night had already aligned, was I really surprised that Brian had guessed the question? Not.

Brian eagerly agreed to be a part of my book. Susan, still a bit drained after reliving the hospital moment, allowed Brian to speak for her as well.

Meeting Brian and Susan that night was indeed no accident. Furthermore, it was no accident that Brian persisted in striking up a conversation with me. Granted, at the time, neither of us was aware of the higher reasons behind his actions, but there was certainly a greater presence directing the events of that night. Maybe Marty had a hand in it. Maybe her story was her way of telling people that our departed loved ones are always with us.

Believe what you want. All I know is that I followed Spirit's directions that night and was greatly rewarded by meeting Brian and Susan (and Alex and Marty).

Marty's story lives on....

Brian

My son Alex ... seeing my reflection in his face, in his spirit and personality. He has an uncanny ability to make everyone he meets smile. His face, his body, his spirit are everything I hope to see in the mirror. I'm his hero and he is mine!

My Southern Crawl

I lived in the South for the first twenty-three years of my life, so one would think that I had ample opportunity to visit a lot of southern states. Unfortunately, that was not the case. You see, my family didn't travel much when I was young. Even though I always wanted to explore what the South had to offer, by the time I was on my own at eighteen, my world revolved around working my way through college. Any extra money went toward food and rent, so travel was a luxury I simply couldn't afford.

Later, when money was more plentiful, it seemed that I always had reason to choose other vacation destinations instead of fulfilling my desire to explore more of the South. However, all excuses and reasons for not exploring my homeland immediately vanished once I was set free from my job. While I was still in the mode of taking advantage of my time away from work, I jumped at the opportunity to finally take a crawl around the South during the spring of 2004.

I covered much ground during my two-week *Thelma and Louise* adventure (my rental car played the role of Thelma). I traveled through such towns as Baton Rouge, Louisiana; Natchitoches, Louisiana (where the movie *Steel Magnolias* was filmed); Mobile, Alabama; Gainesville, Florida; Savannah, Georgia; Charlotte, North Carolina; and Charleston, South Carolina.

Exploring these areas provided a welcome contrast to my daily life in the heavily populated and all-too-hectically paced Southern California. My new surroundings offered a much slower and tranquil lifestyle, and I was very aware that my body was embracing the pace.

Several times along my southern route, I traveled on long stretches of country roads bordered only by acres and acres of uninhabited land that reached out to meet the horizon. Time seemed to pass more slowly, and I thought I sensed less stress in the air, even in the cities.

Oddly enough, even though I haven't lived in the South for over twenty years, I still consider it to be my home. I guess it falls under the heading of "you can take the girl out of the South, but you can't take the South out of the girl."

Now don't get me wrong. I love living in Southern California (my second home). However, the contrast between these two worlds grew bigger every day until it ignited the beginnings of an internal dialogue: Where will I choose to live out the last decades of my life? Is the spirit of this trip influencing me to start thinking of the South as a possible retirement destination? After so many years of swearing off the South, is its grace and beauty now softening my heart? Go figure.

My southern crawl lived up to everything that I had imagined it would be, with one major exception. Initially, I planned the trip with the full intention of adding a dash of southern spice to my book by obtaining answers from people I would meet along the way. However, my trip ended up being more of a search for the perfect retirement spot rather than a search for the meaning of life. Coincidence?

Throughout the trip, I was fully aware that I was connecting more with the places I toured rather than with the people. Several times along the way I asked for Spirit's guidance: Am I missing out on a great opportunity? Should I focus my energy on my book?

I was not surprised by Spirit's first answer. *This is happening for a reason. Go with it.* Even I scratched my head upon hearing this.

When I connected with the moment, I knew the most important thing was to stay true to my book. I figured that since I hadn't been connecting with people during the trip, it wasn't right to start randomly selecting people off the street just to get a head count for my book. It would mean nothing if I started to dishonor my book's original purpose, which was to capture the beauty of a connection that was made during a spontaneous moment. So, that was that.

Spirit then delivered the last part of His answer. *You'll just have to make another southern crawl one day.*

Oh, shucks!

Now, having said all of that, there were two souls from this trip who literally leaped onto my path. I ask you, how could I resist a leaping soul?

It was lunchtime when I reached the city limits of Opelousas, Louisiana. There were not many billboards along the country road into town, but the one for Ray's Diner looked nice enough to convince my growling stomach to follow the directions.

The diner's tall sign on the corner of the property told me I had arrived at the right location, but the gas pumps lined up in front of a mini-mart confused me. I sat in my car for a few minutes looking for another building that might be the diner, but there were none. I was urged by the vibration of my hunger pains to go exploring.

My hesitant footsteps brought me to the mini-mart's checkout counter. Standing watch behind the counter were two women, a teenager and an older-sister-looking woman with a kind face. Both of them tossed me an inquisitive look, but it was the older woman's watchful eyes that locked on mine. Although she looked friendly, her focused eyes seemed to say, "you're not from these parts, are you?"

Only seconds past, but it felt like our locked gaze lingered for several minutes. What was it about this woman that held my eyes on her? With yet another stomach growl, the "spell" was broken and I blinked in the direction of the teenaged girl and asked to be seated.

After filling my tummy with a delicious plate of catfish, I asked my young waitress to speak to the manager. I didn't know why at the time, but I just knew that I wanted to have an answer in my book from someone at the diner.

"The manager won't be back for another hour," said the waitress said with a drawl. "But let me see if the owner is here."

Minutes later, she returned. "Sorry. No one's here to help you."

A gnawing feeling would not allow me to accept that answer, and I took another shot. After giving the waitress a quick explanation about the nature of my book, her expression changed as if a light bulb had gone off in her head.

"Oh, you'll want to talk to Miss Sarah," she offered with a smile. "She's been here forever and knows everything. Wait here and I'll get her."

Mission accomplished.

"Here she is," said the waitress.

I turned around and found myself looking back into the eyes of the same woman I had locked eyes with when I arrived. *Of course it's you I would speak with.* Somehow it all made sense.

After Miss Sarah gave me her answer, we chatted for a long time about life like we were old girlfriends catching up after years spent apart. Better yet, we spoke to each other like two connected souls who immediately recognized the other upon sight. Yes, that's how it was. I hated to leave her.

Miss Sarah

> The result of the culture that we live in … family, friends, and people who we come in contact with. It is grabbing hold of the past and reaching toward the future, while living in the present. It is a combination of what we feel, our spiritual awareness, and how we cope with all of the diversity around us. Life is what we can believe. It is like watching history unfold, being part of something that has no end.
>
> Life is learning to love and grow and reach out to others, changing lives of others as we meet them along the way. Exchanging cultures and ideas and looking to become greater than those left behind.

My day ended in Natchitoches, Louisiana, where my nephew Adam was attending college. Excited as Adam was to see me, he was equally excited to introduce me to "Doc" (Tom), his English professor who had mentored Adam throughout his college years.

The three of us spent the afternoon in deep conversation that continued later over a quiet lakeside dinner. Before the night ended, I expressed my gratitude to Tom for the guidance and friendship showed to Adam. The best form of appreciation I could offer was to ask for his answer to the meaning of life question, which he graciously provided.

In the spring of 2006, Tom unexpectedly passed away. Heart broken like most students, Adam told me that one reason students took the loss so hard was because had it not been for Tom's dedication, a lot of students would not have seen their graduation day.

Tom

> Life is a series of steps. And if we are lucky, we meet each day head on with our attitudes du jour—good, bad, indifferent, apathetic, loving, spiteful, gracious, unkind—whatever. And all we need to do is manage to put one foot in front of the other and walk the path that has been marked for that day, that night, that moment, always with an eye on the past events and an ear to the ground. But always being engaged and conscious of interpersonal, societal, cultural, and spiritual facets that can make a day in the life a brilliant diamond or a chunk of cubic zirconium.
>
> To make life have meaning, all we need do is put one foot in front of the other and walk forward into the realities we call life. From these diverse, converging realities, we construct life ... we give it meaning.

I Promise ... This Will Be My Last Trip

Steve (my musician friend that you met earlier) is from Connecticut, and for the past twenty years or so, he and I have had the same conversation regarding the locale of his childhood. It goes something like this:

"You know, I have always wanted to visit New England to see the change of colors. Let's go leaf peeping," I say.

And every year, Steve replies, "I would love to show you the area and take you along the back country roads that you have only seen in pictures."

"Yes, one day we will have to do that," I then say, ending the conversation in the usual way.

Well, sometime in early 2004, I changed my closing remark to this yearly conversation.

"Enough is enough," I declared. "We've been saying the same thing over and over for years. Let's just pick a week, book it, and plan our lives around it."

I'm happy to say that we did just that.

The scenery in the New England states was absolutely magnificent, one of those you-gotta-see-it-to-believe-it places. Words and pictures all but fail to truly describe the beauty of experiencing it firsthand. I walked away from my love affair with New England with an eyeful of beauty, a heart filled with love, and a peaceful mind.

The best part of the trip was meeting Steve's family and friends. After some twenty years of knowing Steve, this was the first time meeting anyone from his East Coast family.

Everyone in Steve's circle of family and friends was absolutely fabulous and welcomed me with open arms. If not for the fact that they were bona fide Yankees, I would jokingly say that they demonstrated true southern hospitality. Their spirit of love and generosity didn't at all surprise me because Steve has a gift for attracting into his life only the most loving people.

Gee, have I "accidentally" included myself in that lot? Hey, it's my book, and I will do what I like!

Once again, I was shown that the world is chock-full of loving spirits, and our goal as human beings is to make sure that the distance that separates us from other loving spirits is only measured by miles and not by our level of intolerance.

Gina

> The meaning of life to me is waking up every day to a wonderful life that I have had for my fifty-two years. Having a great husband and family means everything to me. Just enjoy life to the fullest and never ever take it for granted.

Tony

> Having good friends, good music, and a love of entertainment. I like to be funny like wisecracking and busting balls with the guys at the mall.

Dave

> Family, friends, sunlight, ocean, music, adventure, and the love and pursuit of all ...

Michael

This is a question that I have pondered for many years, yet the answer has forever eluded me. My philosophy has always been that it is a precious gift and should be treated as such. With the dawning of every day, a fresh palette is placed before us, affording every one the opportunity to create, discover, and ultimately experience all that it has to offer. However, in the final analysis, it would be fair to reason ... we are life, and life is what we make it.

JoEllen

Simply stated: life is a journey through the universe. The contacts and contributions throughout it define our existence.

OK, I Lied

I took one more trip before looking for one of those jobby things again. I returned to Hawaii in the fall of 2004.

There really is no need for me to ramble on about how wonderful and beautiful most everything is in Hawaii. If you've been there, then you already know what I speak of. And if you haven't been there, then I will just say that the islands of Hawaii are as beautiful and the people as friendly as you have heard.

Knowing that my days of freedom were coming to an end, I wanted to use this trip as a way to celebrate the success of my new chapter. I also wanted to savor every moment because I knew that once I returned to work, my next vacation would be a long ways away (well maybe, maybe not).

The one thing that I didn't want to do on this final trip was work on my book. But as fate (and my life) goes, when I noticed a particularly joyful soul jumping onto my path, I couldn't resist scooping her up into the fold.

Jamy

> Finding my inner peace. Weird thing is ... I've already found it. I have a great job, a loving and caring hubby, and the most beautiful daughter in the world. Without them, my life would be nothing.

Rejection City

At this point in my new chapter, it had been over two years since Spirit's first words were spoken in my heart.

This is only a new chapter in your life. You hold the pen; I'll guide your hand. And together, we'll write one hell of a chapter.

I stayed true to those words and chose to make my book a reality.

My first step was to try to find a literary agent to help sell my book to a traditional publisher. But after receiving enough rejection letters to wallpaper my office, I came to believe what is already widely known in publishing: agents reject about 99 percent of the queries they receive.

I am not alone.

I knew that I was a long way away from being discouraged. I mean really, was I going to let a three-inch stack of "Dear Author" rejection letters get me down? I had Spirit on my side and knew with all my heart that my book was going to be published one day—no matter what.

So I breathed in Spirit … mentally thanked everyone for sending me a rejection letter … and registered for the 2005 Santa Barbara Writers Conference.

Long story short, the conference was worth every dime and every second of my time. Even though I felt like a fraud, it was thrilling to be immersed in such a creative environment, and at the same time, humbling to be surrounded by so many fabulous undiscovered writers.

Lori Gervasi, author of *Fight Like a Girl*

God. It is all about Him. In the beginning it was, and at the end it will be again. There really is nothing else. This is what I surrender and subscribe to each day and because of Him, I am free. When we give ourselves to Him and to His word, we become the person He intended us to be, and it is always better than what we could've ever imagined.

The meaning of life is to be true to ourselves and our creator. The meaning of life is something we were born with and born for. Him. All the way. There is no meaning without Him.

Eddie

I once thought that the true meaning of life was some lofty unattainable thing so far beyond our grasp as mere humans that we need not try to find the answer. That was before Ron died.

Ron passed out of this world on May 20, 1990. I watched as the AIDS virus, like some invisible vampire, drew out his life force drop by drop. But Ron was never defeated. He lived his life until he died. He laughed and made everyone else laugh. He called friends to give them encouragement. He enjoyed every moment, every chance, every experience. In his dying, he taught me how to live.

I now think that the meaning of life is in getting through it. Getting through it with love and grace ... and a few laughs.

Keith

What you make of it.

Ralph

Philosophers and clergy have been attempting to answer this since the beginning of recorded history. Personally, I try always to be open to all interpretations and slants—not embrace them necessarily but at least consider if the ideas have merit or speak to me.

In truth, we have no way of being certain about what life means. Science teaches us that absolute certainty is not available to humans regarding the understanding of our world.

Like Joseph Campbell, I like to look at religion, folklore, and all things spiritual and cull from them common elements. Those things, and not their differences, would seem closer to the transcendent truth we all seek.

If one leads a mean life, is it as valuable as a Mother Theresa's life? I don't think so. Therefore, I see life as many things. If it's a test or trial, one should seek to make a positive contribution. But deeper than that, we need to follow our internal compass. Seek happiness (not selfishness) because to be happy you must have unity (your inner self is attuned to the outside world). When you are whole, you have a greater capacity to give and create a circle of love, encouragement, etc. Your life will have value.

Is the meaning of life the struggle for value, love? I don't know. But it is the only way to have a good life.

Jennifer

God in you, surrounding you, enveloping the universe, and creating and forming all we know, are, and what we will become. Energy forms that resonate into infinity and beyond. We are all one spirit, and that collective spirit is called life.

At the conference, I had the unique opportunity to speak with literary agents—face-to-face! If I was going to get rejected by this lot, they were going to have to do it to my face; I had had it with the form rejection letter. This was my chance to gain valuable insight into how agents thought.

Surprisingly, all agents were very gracious and thought well of my idea, my writing, and my "voice," but no one was so moved to want to represent me. However, one agent advised that to help sell the book to publishers, it would help tremendously if I included celebrities in my book.

Yikes! Celebrities? My book was personal and filled with heartfelt words from real people with whom I had made a connection. Did I really want to dilute the spirit of my book with answers from Hollywood types? But then I started thinking of the endless list of actors who I've admired over the years. How cool would it be to get their answer?

The answer came soon enough.

Me? A Celebrity Stalker?

Three months after the Santa Barbara Writers Conference, I landed a job selling ad space again. Mind you, it had been three years since I had been set free and living as a free spirit, so going back to work was a huge event in my life.

I promised myself that now that I had a job, I would do my best to continue working on my book. And who knew? Maybe it was the right time to follow the literary agent's suggestion and begin trying to get celebrities to join my journey. That idea felt good, so I launched the thought into the universe and readied myself to receive its bounty.

It was September 2005, just a few weeks after I started working. I was returning from a trade show in Boston and popped into the airport gift shop to buy a book for the flight home. As I rummaged through my purse for money, I heard his voice.

"Is there ATM machine near here?" he asked the clerk.

The cashier pointed the way and he left. I stood motionless with only one thought skipping across my mind: *Oh my God! He's going to be my first celeb!*

What I did next surprised even me. Yes, I admit it—I stalked him to the ATM machine, but I stood a respectful distance away.

God, I can't believe I'm doing this. I don't do this. I don't "do" the celebrity thing!

And then, Spirit's words calmed me. *Do it for the children.*

Forward. March.

He began walking away from the ATM machine, and I felt Spirit's hand on my back, pushing me to follow him. I sort of lunged in his direction with luggage in tow.

"Excuse me," I said.

"Yes?" he replied, looking directly into my eyes.

"How awful would it be for me to bug you right now?" I asked.

"It depends," he said with an oh-so-cute smile.

I can't believe I'm doing this!

Here was my big chance. Having been in sales for over a decade, I knew that in this moment, I had to deliver the best thirty-second elevator pitch of my life. I launched into the explanation of my book.

"I'm writing a book …" I began, "… and asking celebs to be a part of it."

Somehow I finished the pitch without passing out.

"So what's the question?" he asked.

"Well, I can't tell you until you agree to be in it. It's an all-or-nothing-at-all deal." I silently giggled at myself. Look at me, laying down the law to this celebrity!

"Don't worry. I won't steal the idea," he urged.

His gorgeous eyes won me over. I gave in and told him the question. He thought for a few seconds and began speaking his answer to me. I stopped him in midstream.

"Oh, no," I said, handing him a pen and pad. "You have to write it down for me."

He must have thought I was some kind of pushy broad. Here I was, standing in the middle of Boston Logan airport and telling this celebrity what to do, how to do it, and when to do it.

As he began to write his answer, I saw a woman heading directly for us. *Oh, God. I know this broad thinks this is just about getting an autograph!* In my head, I repeated to her: *Go away! Go away!*

She approached and asked, "Are you Richard Dreyfuss?"

True to his adorable sense of humor, he replied, "No, I'm Tom Cruise."

He still had it.

The lady began yapping her head off while Richard—sorry, Mr. Dreyfuss—attempted to write his answer. I think the commotion made by the woman was a bit distracting because he turned away and headed to a nearby bench to finish his answer.

To the yapping lady, I merely smiled and pretended to listen to her while I chanted *Go away! Go away! Go away!*

She soon tired of waiting for an autograph and simply walked away.

Thank you, God!

Richard returned and looked me dead in the eyes.

"It does," he said, as he handed me his answer.

"Thank you." That's all I could say.

Richard Dreyfuss

> It's your choice. You choose to give meaning or not. If you choose to say life has no meaning, it doesn't. You'd be an idiot, but there you go. If you choose to say it does, it does. (Hint: It does.) It's your choice.

Nine months later, I attended another trade show, this time in Chicago.

When I think of Chicago, two things come to mind: jazz and Italian food. OK, I also think of Oprah. But since I hadn't received a dinner invitation from her, I knew my first night in town would involve a plate of pasta and some cool tunes.

The question was, where would I go to hear the kind of jazz I like? Slow, sensuous, old-fashioned jazz is what I like. Give me a soulful singer purring romantic lyrics any time.

Several jazz clubs were listed in the tourist guide in my hotel room. I read each write-up about three times, but I kept going back to one in particular, a place called Jazz Showcase. For some reason, I didn't trust that selection, so I went back and read each write-up. Again. And once again, I was drawn back to the section on Jazz Showcase. Was I paying attention to what Spirit was trying to tell me? Not.

I called the concierge for a recommendation.

"We have discount coupons to a couple of places in town," he said.

"A discount would be nice," I said, "but wouldn't a place that offers coupons also attract tourists?"

I wanted a place where the locals went for the "real stuff."

The concierge hemmed and hawed a bit, and I could see that he was going to be of no help to me.

Once again, I had a gnawing feeling to go back and read the write-up about Jazz Showcase again. To end the debate once and for all, I decided to call Jazz Showcase for show times and to find out whether there was a good Italian restaurant within walking distance. I was told that Maggiano's was directly across the street. Since I love Maggiano's, that sealed the deal.

It was odd, though. Why didn't I ask what band was playing?

Once inside Jazz Showcase, the décor took me back to a time that I have only seen in old movies. The dimly lit room. The scattering of small candlelit tables. The low murmur of anticipation from the patrons. It all fit the picture of what I imagined a jazz club of the thirties or forties would be like.

From the back of the club, a man gingerly strolled by my table.

"Are you writing a letter?" asked the man with smiling eyes.

"No," I drawled. "Just doing some journaling. But I am writing a book, so pass by on your way back."

Good Lord. Why on Earth did I say that to him? I was still adamant about not wanting to tell anyone about my book until we'd made a connection of sorts. With this man, I had barely laid eyes on him let alone make a connection. Obviously I was going against my own wishes. So what was it about him that made me tell him about my book?

I watched to see where in the audience this man was seated. Boy, was I surprised to see the gentleman walk onto the softly lit stage and take his seat behind the piano.

The crowd hushed. The smiling eyed man counted off—"a one and a two"—and the group's slow, sensual style of music began to gently float over the candlelit room. I was in heaven. The moment was filled with everything I had asked for, plus an additional treat: the stranger with the smiling eyes was also the lead singer.

His voice was rich and smooth, yet rough and complex at the same time. Every word he sang was strong and deliberate, yet gentle. As he caressed the ivories, his command over the keys was obvious, but his touch was so tender. Every velvety note from the stranger's throat resonated in my soul and allowed me to sink deeper into a melodious trance. *Thank you, God, for sending me here.*

As I listened to the music, my mind replayed what all had happened for me to land in this particular moment, in this particular place. I knew that this all was just another sign that when we "put it out there" and listen to Spirit, we usually get what we want. Eventually.

No matter how many times I experience this sort of thing, I'm always left with feelings of awe of how the world works and how lucky I am—more accurately, how blessed I am. How wonderful my life is when I listen to Spirit. Fanning these thoughts caused emotion to rise up, and I began to cry. Then suddenly, I could feel Daddy at my side and greeted him.

I giggled to myself and asked Daddy, *So you like this kind of jazz, too?* I never knew that. How much didn't I know about him.

I thought about how wonderful it would be if Daddy were indeed sitting next to me, enjoying this moment. I cried even more.

After the band's set was over, I approached the smiling-eyed man.

"Your music makes a woman's heart cry," I said

"Oh, oh," he said with concern.

"Oh, no, no. It's a good thing," I quickly replied. "Your music just really touched my heart."

Before he had a chance to think that I was a total loon, I introduced myself and offered a quick rundown of my book. I explained that the experiences I write about have come from listening to and following Spirit, and that by following this path, I'm able to make a connection of spirit with the "strangers" I meet.

With his eyes fixed on mine, he listened to my story and nodded in agreement.

"That's what I try to do with my music," he said. "Every time I play, I try to have the music come from my heart and hope that it will touch someone."

"Well, darlin', I'm here to tell you that your music touched this woman's heart, so much so that it made me cry."

He was too busy to take part in my book that night, but he gave me his cell phone number and asked me to call him in a couple of weeks.

"I *will* call you," I said as I gazed into his smiling eyes and waved good-bye.

Weeks later, in preparation for the call, I Googled the man's name to learn more about his band. He had told me that they had played in my area before, and I was curious to see whether they were coming back to my neighborhood any time soon.

The Google listings appeared before my eyes, and I gasped.

"I'm so embarrassed," I exclaimed over the phone to my sister Diane. "Oh my God! I didn't know who he was when I talked to him in Chicago. I hadn't put two and two together."

Here I am, a jazz lover, and I had been clueless as to whom I was about to call.

The man with the smiling eyes was none other than Freddy Cole, brother of Nat King Cole and uncle to Natalie Cole.

Now it all made sense. As I thought back on the events of that night in Chicago, I realized that Spirit had been in charge from the very beginning. In fact, Spirit had delivered me to everything I had asked for and more. Great Italian food. The style of jazz I love. The perfect intimate setting. A "visit" with Daddy. And a celebrity to boot.

But most of all, I knew the one thing that I was most grateful for was having had the opportunity to listen to Freddy's music with an honest ear—meaning that when I listened to his music that night, I wasn't thinking of Freddy's family tree. I wasn't comparing his sound to anyone else. Instead, I had been given the opportunity to be touched by the spirit of Freddy's music.

Another connection of spirit with a "stranger" was granted.

Lionel "Freddy" Cole

Learning how to live it. Now. A lot of people never learn how to do it. A lot of people live on yesterday not realizing that today and tomorrow is a gift. That's what I call living for life.

The Ripple Effect

I love the concept that what you put out in the universe comes back to you tenfold. I'm not sure where this concept originated, but I latched onto it decades ago and have since turned it into a guiding principle in my life. Sure, I admit that I use it for purely selfish reasons: if I do good deeds in life, then I will receive good deeds, tenfold. I like that idea.

Fortunately—or unfortunately, depending on your viewpoint—there is always balance in life, meaning that the flip side of this tenfold concept eventually holds true as well. In other words, if you do bad things in life, you better duck when it hits the fan. Since I try to stay on the good side of life, I keep my focus more on the positive aspect of this concept.

My mind works in an odd fashion. When a thought or concept enters my head, a mental image is usually attached to it. So when I think about doing good in life, the image that comes to mind is that of ripples in a pond.

We've all tossed a pebble into the middle of a pond and watched as the ripples spread out across the water and then quickly disappeared. Small pebble, small ripples. Simple enough, right? But did you know that one small pebble can create ripples that last for days?

On a trip to New York City, June 2006, a "good-deed pebble" was tossed my way. See if you can count the number of "ripples" that occurred as a result.

I'm one of those travelers who simply must have an aisle seat on the plane—not because I have long legs but because I drink so much water and have to "go" so often. If I didn't sit near the aisle, I would end up feeling awful for having to constantly bother people to let me out of the row. So having an aisle seat is really a *thing* for me.

On this particular flight, I boarded early and was the first to arrive in the row of seats. I was assigned the middle seat. Yes, the middle seat. But you know what? It was OK with me. *Huh! That's odd. I'm really OK with having the middle seat.* Next to arrive was the window gal, and then the aisle guy.

Now, most frequent flyers know that you must establish the game rules with your seatmates early on in the flight. Long story short: if you want to be left alone, as in "don't bother me," you must pull out your reading materials right away and keep your nose buried there for the duration of the flight. I confess that there have been a few times when I've whipped out a book to avoid the in-flight chatting. But not this time. Instead, I quickly began a conversation with window gal. *Had I not given her enough time to pull out her reading materials?*

Window gal Stacy began telling me all about her job as an event planner and about all the celebrities that she had recently met. *Celebrities? Bingo!*

"I should hire you to help me with my book," I said with a chuckle, and then launched into a brief explanation.

We spoke for only a few minutes when I noticed Stacy reaching for her computer. I took this as her way of saying *Don't bother me anymore.*

Out of respect, I ended the conversation by saying "If you are interested, let me know before we land so that I can ask you my question." I then pulled out my reading materials as a sign of solidarity.

But come to find out, I was wrong about the reason Stacy grabbed her computer. She actually wanted to help my efforts in reaching celebrities.

"This may help you get in touch with celebrities," she said. "Take down this information."

Oh my God! I was shocked by the information she gave me. How sweet she was to trust me with it. I made a mental note that when I did begin the work on the celebrity version of my book, I would be sure to thank her in the dedication.

As a side note: is it just me, or does anyone else think it a bit coincidental that the other gal I met on a plane (in "Gifts From Above") was also named Stacy? Just a thought.

Stacy

> So many make this complicated when you look at what is truly important. I have found that the meaning of life is simply to live.
>
> For those that need explanation, I say open your doors and windows and go into the world and experience, share and lose yourself in the present. I see so many who lock their doors and move in shadows ... the shadows will take everything if you allow it. So for the person still searching and seeking out the answer to this question, I say STOP ... it's time to live today with the sunlight.

I boarded the second leg of my flight to New York, spotted my *aisle* seat, and said hello to the lady seated by the window. I was ready to hoist my bag in the overhead bin when she waved her boarding pass in front of me.

"My husband and I got separated," she said. "Would you change seats with him?"

She pointed to the man waving in the back of the plane.

She added, "He has an aisle seat!"

Now how did she know about my thing with aisle seats?

"Sure, not a problem."

They were most appreciative.

I arrived at my new aisle seat and began to settle in. Bag in the overhead bin? Check. Pillow for my back? Check. Reading materials? Check. I was all set.

"Hi, I'm there," the man said as he pointed to the window seat.

We exchanged pleasantries and then buckled up.

Only a few seconds passed when the man turned to me.

"My wife and I got separated ... our seats aren't together," he said as he pointed to a lady waving at us from the front of the plane. "Would you mind changing seats with her?"

Again? I smiled, and I think he knew what I was thinking.

He quickly added, "She has an aisle seat!"

This time I played hardball for the exchange.

"Well, OK. I'll change seats on one condition. You have to bring my bag up to me when we land."

"Deal," he said with a relieved grin.

I retraced my steps to the front of the plane, all the while thinking that somewhere down the road I would receive something good in return for my good deeds. Selfish thinking? Well, I like to think of it as living a balanced life. Both of the couples I exchanged seats with got what they wanted. Now I was ready to receive the good from my actions. Balance. Works for me!

Since I wasn't on a tight schedule, I took my time getting off the plane. A trip to the ladies' room. A casual stroll through the airport. And then I reached the shuttle van reservation desk.

A large group of people waited alongside the reservation desk. Did this mean I had a long wait ahead of me? (Sometimes you have to wait up to twenty minutes for a shuttle van.) I stood in the reservations line for only a few seconds when the shuttle driver approached.

"Where're you going?" he asked.

"Manhattan. Midtown."

"Come with me."

Yippee! I didn't have to wait.

I immediately said to myself: *You see there. You did a good deed by changing seats with those two couples on the plane, and already you received something good in return.* I was a happy camper, satisfied knowing that the world was a balanced place.

But was this the only good thing that was in store for me?

The shuttle van was filled to the brim—about twelve passengers in all. With a quick survey, I knew that having so many people on board meant the van was going to make at least six or seven stops. *Oh, Lordy, it will be midnight before I get to my hotel.*

At the van's first stop, only one man was dropped off. Not a good start. There were way too many of us left. *Breathe, Louise. Just breathe.*

We arrived at the second stop. It was *my* hotel! Yes, I was the second stop. I silently shouted *Thank you, God!* Again I thought, *You get what you give. I did good, and I am receiving good. Life is good!*

But did good things stop happening there? I think not.

I arrived at the hotel registration desk. There was no line. *Thank you, God.*

I walked into my room. It was beautiful.

I looked out the window. My room had a view of the river. I laughed with joy and shouted out loud, "Thank you, God!"

I ordered room service. Put on my new Freddy Cole CD (*This Love of Mine*). Unpacked my bag. Laid out my toiletries. Ironed all my shirts for my three-day stay in the city.

Almost an hour had passed, and my food still hadn't arrived. I knew the food was long overdue because Freddy was no longer singing to me. Instead, it was now my stomach that was singing loud and clear. I called room service and politely inquired after my food.

"Oh, I'm so sorry," the attendant said. "I'm not sure what is wrong with the chef tonight. To make up for the wait, your dinner is on the house."

He continued, "And do you drink wine? Let me bring you a glass of wine. On me."

At this point, having received all of these good turns, I could have almost kissed those couples on the plane for asking me to change seats with them.

But did it stop there? I think not. I continued to receive gifts throughout my stay in New York.

The Neighborhood of 9/11

From the very start, I knew that I wanted to dedicate a chapter of my book to New York firefighters and their families, particularly those touched by 9/11. I mean really, who better to have an answer to the meaning of life than the people who deal with life-threatening events every day of their lives.

A couple of weeks prior to my trip to New York, I told my sister Diane that I was going to name the chapter "The Neighborhood of 9/11."

"I thought you wanted the chapter to be just with firefighters," she inquired.

"Yeah, I know. I can't say why, but I just know that it has to be called 'the neighborhood.'"

To kick off this chapter, I decided to give a small shout-out to the local fire-fighting heroes in my own neighborhood.

Bill

> The meaning of life to me is found in my relationship with God. Through my faith, I have found the true meaning of what it is to be a father, friend, and a child of God. My faith is something to be shared with family, friends, and fellow firefighters.
>
> The meaning of life is taking what God has given to you and using it to serve Him. We all have talents; we all have the ability to help others. I have been blessed to have been in the fire service for over twenty-five years, helping others and serving God as a firefighter.

Don

> Life is created by God, and I believe that the meaning would be
> to serve God. I believe that I was called to protect people, and
> that's why I worked hard to become a firefighter, but all the doors
> were opened by God along the way. So in essence, I believe the
> meaning of life is to serve God and each other in whatever capac-
> ity you are called to. Through this process, God is perfecting us
> for the life after this one.

To prepare for this chapter, I did a bit of research and spoke with
someone in the press office of the New York City Fire Department
(FDNY). I wanted to make sure that I followed proper procedure
from the get-go. The press office told me that although they couldn't
officially endorse my efforts or organize anything for me, it was OK
for me to find off-duty firefighters and ask them for answers.

The first place I researched was the firehouse directly across the
street from the World Trade Center site.

From my web search, I learned that the law firm of Holland &
Knight had donated to this firehouse a solid bronze sculpture—fifty-
six feet long by six feet high—that depicted the fire department personnel who responded to the World Trade Center disaster.

What did this piece of information have to do with me? Well, the
memorial dedication was on the same weekend I was scheduled to be
in New York, and the ceremony would take place at the same firehouse I had planned to contact. Coincidence? I think you know my
answer to that question by now.

It was a rainy Thursday morning when I set out for "the neighborhood of 9/11."

"I'm going to the World Trade Center site," I told the taxi driver
outside my hotel.

I watched the sites of New York whiz by my window, feeling
excited, confused, and amazed all at the same time. Here I was, alone
in New York City, about to walk up to the front door of the firehouse

and say, "Hi. My name is Louise. Would you be in my book?" Would they think I was crazy? Would they laugh at me? The very thought of what I was about to do made me laugh. And then I cried.

Morning traffic caused a little delay in arriving at the site. I took advantage of the extra time and started breathing deeply to release my nervous feelings. On the last exhale, I noticed my cab driver for the first time.

I always love to read the names of my cab drivers from the posted driver's licenses. I particularly love reading names that are foreign to my world. Such was the case with my Thursday morning cab driver, Abdelhak Snaky.

Since I love to travel, I stared at his name and tried to image where he was from. My mind filled with exotic, faraway places. Places I wanted to see some day.

"You (expletive) jerk!" he shouted as a pedestrian darted in front of the car. "They don't think anything about just jumping in your way." He waved his arm wildly in the air.

This made me giggle.

In an apologetic voice, he offered, "New Yorkers can be so rude. They think nothing about flipping you off. Even when they're in the wrong."

He knew firsthand the challenge of driving in New York. I, myself, did not have the courage to even attempt to drive in the city, but listening to Snaky's heated passion and frustration made me laugh at myself. Here I was … in New York … listening to a venting cab driver. I saw it all as one big adventure, and I loved it.

I tried to change the energy in the car, so I asked about his name. We shared a giggle over the pronunciation.

"Snaky is my last name," he said, "and people call me by Snaky."

I tried it out. "Snake-y?"

"Oh, no, no," he giggled, "The *a* is not a long *a*. I'm not a snake."

As you may have guessed by now, I love talking to people and learning more about them. Since traffic continued to hold us captive, Snaky was all mine.

I learned that Snaky spoke fluent French. He had lived in Morocco and in Paris, moved to New York City in 1996, and was currently studying to be a personal trainer.

"I just passed my citizenship test," he beamed. "I am waiting to be sworn in."

I know it may sound crazy, but in that moment, I was so very proud of him and admired his courage. For what little I knew of his life, he had already accomplished so much.

Could I, couldn't I? Should I, shouldn't I? I asked myself. Did I have the courage to ask Snaky to be in my book? Spirit gave me the answer.

"Snaky, are you in a hurry?" I grinned.

"After you, I'm going to the airport for fares. But, no, I'm in no hurry," he said with an inquisitive look in the rear view mirror.

Well, that was all I needed to hear. When we reached my destination, he pulled to the curb and we sat for several minutes while I explained my book. Without hesitating, he wrote his answer.

I don't care where you are born or what you do for a living or the status of your green card. Snaky's answer was universal and timeless.

I thanked Snaky for his answer and told him how wonderful it was to meet him. Before I left the cab, I shared a bit of advice.

"It is your job to spread joy. Teach by example. So the next time you get flipped off, just simply smile and wave at the person. And send out a prayer for them. One day, they'll catch on."

Abdelhak Snaky

> Life for me is to be humble, nice with everybody, and also help someone if they need help. And also enjoy it.

After walking a block or two, I arrived at the firehouse. I stood in front of the building and gazed at its façade, not knowing what was my next step.

The face of the building looked like a solid, windowless wall of steel, impenetrable as Fort Knox. Where was the welcome mat? The only thing I could see at the front door was a security keypad that seemed to say "Don't even think about knocking on our door!" *What am I supposed to do now?*

My feet couldn't move as if they were frozen in mud. My heart raced with nervous tension. Would I chicken out and run away? I had not come all this distance just to walk away, but I didn't know my next move. So I just stood there. Seconds passed. Minutes passed. I breathed in my surroundings and gazed over the area where the Twin Towers once stood. All the while, I knew in my heart that I was supposed to be there. So I waited. And waited.

I guess about five (long) minutes passed, when the front door of the firehouse swung open and a stream of workers and firehouse personnel filed passed me. *Now what do I do?*

They walked passed me, turned the corner, and stopped in front of a wall covered in taped brown paper. A few workers peeled back a corner of the brown paper that concealed the bronze plaque that was to be revealed at the dedication in two days. *Look at me. Standing in front of this firehouse. Being one of the first people in the world to lay eyes on this great monument. Is life cool, or what? But now what do I do?*

I stood on the corner of the firehouse for several more minutes, gathering Spirit's advice on how to proceed.

A lone straggler filed out the door. And with Spirit's gentle push, my feet were freed from my post. I approached the firefighter.

"Hi, my name is Louise," I started.

I think my nerves had control over my brain in that moment because I can't recall exactly what I said. But I do know that I explained to the man that I was writing a book and dedicating a chapter to the neighborhood of 9/11.

"Sorry. We can't talk to the press," he explained very nicely.

Inside, I giggled slightly. Me? Part of the press?

"Oh, I'm nobody like that." In case he meant that they weren't allowed to talk about the events of 9/11, I added, "And my book isn't about 9/11."

"Nah, we'd get in trouble. We can't talk to anyone." He walked away and joined the group peeking at the memorial.

Now, you would think that I would be really bummed about hearing this news. Disappointed? Yes. Surprised? No. Instead, I had clarity. I finally understood why I had told Diane my chapter would have to be on the "neighborhood" of 9/11. It all made sense

But what should I do now? Do I roam the streets saying "Hi, I'm Louise. Would you be in my book?" Would people laugh at me? Would they think I was a loon? I knew these thoughts were coming from Ego, so I decided to ignore the fear that was trying to take hold of me. Instead, I chose to listen to Spirit.

Louise, you know why you're doing this. Yes, you think what you are attempting is merely a small gesture. But you also live by the Truth that everyone must do what they can to help others and help make this world a better place. Your dedicated chapter is your gift to the "the neighborhood." Such a gift will not be laughed at.

Once again, Spirit's words gave me the courage and strength to begin my neighborhood adventure. For the next two days, I walked the neighborhood and asked certain people to be in my book. My first one was from John.

Before 9/11, John's cafe was called The Food Exchange. And for three months following 9/11, his cafe served as a makeshift hospital.

While speaking with John, I don't remember breathing. I was too busy hanging onto every word of his story of that awful day. John knew many, many people who were lost to the tragedy.

I will never know what John's eyes saw or experience the weight of the memories his heart must carry. All I know is that just sitting in his presence was an honor. I wanted to cry but thought it disrespectful. Why should he have to deal with my sorrow as well?

My mind filled with questions as I watched John write his answer. How does he manage to get through each day? Where does he get the courage to just put one foot in front of the other? How could he walk through his cafe each day and not remember? I wasn't there, so it all will remain beyond my comprehension.

As I left, I could only thank God to be able to walk on such hallowed ground. No words, just honor and respect for those who continue to survive 9/11 every day.

John Costalas—owner, Essex World Cafe

> I worked and lived near the Trade Center for more than thirty-five years. When the first tower came down, I was sixty yards away. God was with me, and I came out alive. Every day after 9/11, I met people who were very close to me; they had lost some loved ones. Then I knew what life is. After 9/11, I appreciate every day more than before and I enjoy life *more!*

I saw the Pussycat Lounge from across the street and giggled at the thought of having such an establishment in my book. What, the meaning of life is going see a girly show? I don't think so!

As I crossed the street and walked toward the club, I scolded myself for making such snap judgments. *Who the heck are you to say, Louise? What nerve.*

Nevertheless, I chose to walk on by.

I walked no farther than two or three steps past the front entrance when I was stopped cold. By who? By what? I didn't know. All I knew was that, once again, my feet were frozen in mud. I stood still for a few seconds. Took a deep breath. Smiled a knowing smile, and walked right up to the well-dressed gentleman posted at the front door of the Pussycat Club.

OK, I admit it. Upon approach, my judgmental mind kicked in once again: *This is New York. No one has time for some Pollyanna like you. Plus, he's sitting in front of a strip club, which is so against your (undefined) feminist beliefs. And, he's a big dude who could squash you with his little pinky.*

Did I really want to take this risk? Thankfully, Spirit slapped me upside my head and told me to behave myself.

"Hi! My name is Louise," I said and then launched into my spiel.

From our short encounter, I could see that Haitian-born Julien had a sweet soul and an internal glow that shined from his eyes. He was what ladies would call a sweet, lovable teddy bear.

He readily agreed to be in my book.

I read his answer and gave him a big smile.

"You just did. You just helped me. Thank you!" I said.

Suddenly, a man hurriedly approached from the street, interrupting our good-byes.

"Can I park there? Is it OK if I park there? Will I get towed? I'll only be a minute. Can I park here?" he asked without taking a breath.

Julien, with his sweet nature all aglow, smiled at the frazzled man.

"Sure, sure. It's OK. It's OK."

Julien turned back toward me, and I laughed out loud.

"You just did it again. You helped that man, just seconds after writing that you like helping people."

He humbly shrugged his shoulders.

"You live by your words," I said admiringly with one more "thank you" and a warm handshake.

I walked away, grinning from ear to ear and thinking about instant karma. Was it by accident that I stopped to talk to Julien? Was it by accident that the frazzled man approached us at the very moment that Julien wrote that he liked to help people? Was it the universe making up for the earlier slap in the head, giving me yet another opportunity to see how wrong I am to judge people? All accidents? I think not.

Will I ever walk *into* the Pussycat Club? Respectfully, I think not. (But ya never know!)

Julien

My plan in any life: I like to help people.

◆   ◆   ◆

Gerard

Wealth and family.

William Pierre Dixon—general manager, Suspender Restaurant

The meaning of life is to enjoy and spread joy no matter what the situation throughout life.

◆   ◆   ◆

As I strolled through the neighborhood, I thought about what that firefighter told me about not being allowed to speak to anyone. I wondered whether that rule held true for police officers as well.

Minutes later, two off-duty officers just happened to be seated next to me at lunch.

"Hi, my name is Louise. Can you be civilians right now?" I asked.

"Sure thing," they replied.

And we were off and running.

Bobby Summers

The meaning of life is to live it to its fullest. Enjoy every day, even when things go wrong. The meaning of life is to learn from your mistakes and guide others from your experiences, to have goals and dreams, to enjoy your friends and family, and make every day count.

Buffy Summers

> The meaning of life is different to everyone, of course. For me, it's to be happy. "The hardest thing to do in this world is to live in it." As long as you're happy doing whatever you're doing, you'll be OK.

◆   ◆   ◆

With construction still going on in the neighborhood, I had to walk along some streets under covered walkways. On the wall of a walkway, located across the street from the Trade Center, I came upon this poem. After I read it, my feet wouldn't move until I wrote it down. I sincerely hope the anonymous author doesn't mind that I honor his or her words by including them in my dedication to the neighborhood.

> The Road to Heaven
> While traveling along
> It's never too late
> Take the road that heads to love
> Not the one to hate.
>
> Hate is what took these buildings down,
> With love is how we'll remember those
> No longer around.
>
> Take the right road and you will see,
> How much sweeter life will be.
> The road may be uphill and
> Strewn with stones.
> So get rid of the weight
> And lighten the load.
>
> At the summit there is
> A beautiful view

All of God's peace
Open to you.
—A Police Officer, NYPD

Scott Fryer

Life is a period of time that a person is alive. It is made up of actions, words, and thoughts that determine its quality. A person who is said to be full of life has positive actions, words, and/or thoughts. On the other hand, a person who chooses to dwell on negative actions, words, and thoughts chooses a "hard life."

Usman Ghani

Life means to me what I can give and leave for humanity once I'll expire. I would also add that life is beautiful.

Mayer—manager, Broadway Kosher Cafe

To be good and do good to others so that they can do the proper thing. For example, if someone needs help, financial help, or has a problem in his or her life that you could help, you should do it … as much as you could.

Life is a beautiful thing that was granted to the human race to do their effort to make it to the top by doing kindness and charity to others and yourself, and be always aware of who is watching. You and your deed should be always good in the eyes of other people. We should take it as granted that we are living and we are growing, and we should always think that there is someone that is looking over us.

He is testing us, and we should always be grateful and happy for self and others.

Betsy Chun—owner, World Trade Art Gallery

> As long as God gives me life in this world, I will follow His will
> and love my neighbor.

Nalinee—Corbet & Conley

> Life is a God-given gift. We should appreciate every single breath
> we take, and make the most of whatever we desire.

I loved my experience with security guard Mike because he had me
laughing at him the whole time. From the second he read the question till the time he turned in his answer, he would repeatedly look up
into the air as if waiting for his answer to come floating down from
above. He'd try to gather his thoughts, and then say "Whoa!" He'd
write a few words and repeat "Whoa!" He repeated these steps about
five times.

With a sigh and a chuckle, he handed me his answer. "You got me
thinking!"

Bingo. Exactly my purpose.

Mike Thompson

> The meaning of life to me is enjoying the fresh air. Enjoying the
> ability to be whoever I want to be. To never take life for granted.
> To never settle when it comes to my dreams.

Cosmo Yi—owner, One Way Gift Shop

> Life is trying. We are trying to survive in society where problems
> make people be negative. But, if we try to change the negative
> value to positive, that will be life. Try to be happy. Try to be opti-
> mistic. Try to be polite, and try to be nice to others.

Michael Keane—manager, O'Hara's Restaurant and Pub

> Truthfully, I don't know. Sometimes you wonder what is the meaning of life when you see good happen, and when you see bad happen, you ask what is the purpose. You can't think about it too much, or you'll drive yourself crazy. Is there going to be a reward for those who lead their life the right way?

It was now the end of my second day collecting answers, which meant that it was also my last day in the neighborhood. For my final entry, I wanted the last place I visited to mean something special to the firefighters I was trying to honor in the first place.

I circled back to where my neighborhood visit began—the front corner of the firehouse across from the World Trade Center site. Standing outside were a few firefighters shooting the breeze. I mustered the courage to walk up to one of them.

"Hi, my name is Louise." (I still felt like a nerd saying this.)

Assuring him that I knew of their do-not-talk policy, I asked him a different question: "if there was one place in the neighborhood that is special to this firehouse, what place would that be?"

"O'Hara's!" he shouted before I even finished speaking.

I smiled, happy knowing that I had already obtained an answer from O'Hara's manager, Mike—and happy that I had just been told where I was to end my two-day trip in the neighborhood. O'Hara's was just the place to raise my glass to the honor of having been greeted so warmly by the people I met during my stroll through their neighborhood.

When I walked into O'Hara's, Mike immediately recognized me.

"So, how'd it go?" he asked.

"Good. Really good," I smiled.

I wasn't yet able to put into words the overwhelming feelings born from my experience of the past two days. I merely looked into his eyes and placed my hand over my heart. He understood.

A few minutes later, Mike walked over to me, looked me dead in the eyes, and handed me some sort of book. Before I even looked at what he handed me, I already knew what he was sharing with me.

"This is the photo album of O'Hara's after 9/11," he said, treating it like it was gold.

The album pages were a bit worn from the many hands that had touched it before mine. With each turn of a page, I felt as though everyone who had laid eyes on these pages were sitting next to me. I tried to hold back the emotion that was pounding against my heart, but I failed. I dropped my head and let the tears fall into my lap.

After collecting myself, I handed back the album with the same speechless gesture as before—a grateful look, my hand over my heart, and the unspoken words "Thank you for the honor."

Another guy behind the bar came my way and introduced himself as Jimmy. If memory serves, Jimmy said he had worked at O'Hara's for over eighteen years.

"What's the crowd like here?" I asked him.

"We get everyone from construction guys to Wall Street guys, CEOs and millionaires, all sitting side by side. They all come here."

I knew what he meant because the energy of the place made me feel very welcome.

As I sat at the bar, I filled pages and pages of my journal with the many thoughts and feelings about my time in the neighborhood. During pauses to collect my thoughts, I blindly stared at the TV playing the World Cup.

I drifted away from the TV and into my own mental conversation: How do I put into words the generosity of Spirit that was shown to me during my visit? In a city of rough and tough New Yorkers, how was it that literally everyone I met was so soft and sweet? Have I always misjudged this city? Have I only seen the city through eyes of fear? And more puzzling to me: why was I now feeling such a strong bond with the city?

A loud burst of cheering brought my mind back to the World Cup finals at O'Hara's. Cheering the loudest were two exuberant Ecuadorian fans sitting next to me, Oscar and Mana. The sheer joy on their faces was contagious, and we struck up a conversation.

They enthusiastically agreed to be in my book, but as they read the question, their faces grew solemn. Gone were their joyous smiles.

I learned that Oscar taught school a few blocks away from the World Trade Center site. He was there when the towers fell. The floor on which housed the classrooms didn't have any windows, so the children were spared seeing the towers fall. Unfortunately, their vision could not be spared for long.

Mana then shared her experience of 9/11—the horror of it all, her fear of dying, the terrible sights she witnessed that day. But from all the awful things she saw that day, there was one image in particular that struck her to be out of place: sheets of paper falling from the sky. Sheets of white, crisp paper. Drifting slowly toward the ground as if in slow motion. Each page that fell was in perfect condition. Unscathed. No crinkles. No burn marks. All in perfect condition. She recalled asking: How is this possible?

It was getting late and time for me to leave O'Hara's. I searched for Mike's eyes.

"See you," I said as I waved good-bye, knowing that I would be back ... some day. I walked away wondering if he knew just how much that moment in his bar meant to me.

Oscar Gongora

> Life is something ephemeral: you are here, then you are not. Make a mark. Do something useful so that you can be remembered by someone. Enjoy life to the fullest. Be responsible and learn so you can teach. Enjoy so that you can be happy with your memories. Help so that someone will be grateful to you later on when you need to feel useful. Try to celebrate all the good moments so that you are not down with pessimism. Love your fellow man.

Mana Twing

> When you think you're going to die and your daughter thinks
> you're dead! It happened to me on 9/11. I worked, and still work,
> a block from the towers. 9/11 happened, and my girls thought
> that I was dead. And the worst part, I thought I was going to die,
> too. I knew right away that the meaning of life is my children.

By the time you read this chapter, I will have struggled long and hard
for the proper way, the best way, to end my tribute to those still sur-
viving 9/11 and to those who left in spirit that day. I will simply end
with a request: for all who read this, I ask you to please remember and
honor our heroes who risk their lives for us every day.

A Slice Is a Slice, Right?

The next day was the day of the memorial dedication at the firehouse. Should I return to the neighborhood? The question remained unanswered for only a nanosecond because I knew in my heart this day was for family and friends to honor and remember their loved ones. I felt that it would be disrespectful for me to be in the neighborhood during such a time.

So instead, I made it a "play day." And New York is a wonderful place in which to play. Fabulous museums. Great restaurants. Shopping. Well, I'm not a shopper, but even I know this is the place for fashion.

A warm spring day was the setting for my city adventure. My destination: Central Park. The event: a *Sex and the City* bus tour.

With plenty of time and comfortable shoes, I chose to walk to the park, and along the way, grab a slice of pizza.

My hotel was at Lexington and E. Forty-eighth Street, so there were many routes I could take to get to Central Park. I could stay on Lexington and cross over on E. Sixtieth Street or cross on any of the other numbered streets and then parade down either Madison Avenue or Park Avenue.

With a good idea of the general direction I was headed, I left the hotel lobby and just started walking. I ended up staying on E. Forty-eighth Street. I had no idea why I chose this route.

A few minutes into my walk, sidewalk construction forced me to cross to the other side of the street. Once there, I landed smack in front of the Diamond Café, which had a sign in the window that I wanted to see: "Pizza."

My growling stomach said to go inside ... but was it only my stomach telling me to go in?

With a quick survey of the restaurant, I decided to stay and have a slice.

"A slice of cheese, please," I told the pizza maker.

"OK, sweetie," said the Asian gentleman as I walked away to pay.

When I returned to wait for my slice, a man behind the counter was walking away from the pizza maker, wearing a big grin. He stopped to chat with me.

Still grinning, he explained, "He's learning English, and I was just telling him that calling a lady 'sweetie' is not always appropriate."

"Are you the owner?" I asked.

"Yep. I'm Paul."

"Well, I'm OK with being called 'sweetie,'" I said. "As long as he doesn't call me 'ma'am.' That makes me feel way too old." I giggled and waited for my slice to be ready.

"One slice of cheese," called the pizza maker.

"Thank you, *sweetie*," I replied with a wink, and the three of us had a good laugh.

Folding over my slice of pizza like the locals do, I watched the owner fix his lunch and then watched as he walked over to my table and plopped down in the chair next to me.

Why had he done this?

"What are you doing in town?" he asked.

I explained my book and told him that I had just spent two days collecting answers from the neighborhood of 9/11.

He hesitated in thought for a few seconds. "Funny you should be talking to *me*."

OK, here we go! I sensed that I was about to learn the reason I had chosen my route that day. And I was also about to learn the reason that he had sat down beside me. *Thank you for the quick answers, God!*

He continued, "My original store was across the street from the twin towers."

I smiled, silently saying to myself, *Of course it was. Why else would I have been sent here!*

"I had stayed around once the towers were hit and then ran inside into an elevator shaft when they came down. Two other people were with me in there," he said staring off into the distance. "They both died of suffocation."

Silence.

He slowly added, "I guess God doesn't want me now."

Staring down at my pizza, I asked a final question. "Why didn't you reopen in the neighborhood?"

"Well, there were some landlord disputes, I guess ..." his words trailed off. "But really, I wasn't ready to return."

Without saying a word, I slid a sheet of paper in front of him, and he began writing his answer to my question.

Paul Previti, owner, Diamond Café

> First, you must learn right from wrong. Then decide how often you will do both. Where you end up after making your choices will determine how your life will be!

Ask and Ye Shall Receive

I wanted to end my last night in New York with a nice glass of wine and a few minutes with my journal. I know, not a very exiting choice for a Saturday night in New York City, but I had a very early flight home the next day.

How about going to the W hotel? I've never been there, I asked myself.

Spirit piped in. *Nope, you're going to the Waldorf Astoria.*

The Waldorf it is, I conceded, knowing full well it was best to follow Spirit's words. And really, why on Earth would I argue about going to the Waldorf Astoria?

There is something very special about walking into such a beautiful, posh hotel. Merely walking through the doors that night put me in a good mood. It also made me feel like I should have gone home to change into better clothes.

Off the lobby was the Bull and Bear lounge. I peeked in from the entrance and thought it was pretty, but unfortunately, it was also very busy and noisy inside. I was in the mood for a place a bit more intimate and quiet. My feet dragged a bit as I walked past its entrance, but I proceeded through the lobby to find the ladies' room and an ATM.

At the other end of the hotel was a lovely, sprawling lobby lounge, complete with live piano music and a singer. Live music ... right up my alley! This was my place.

Nope, you're not staying here. Go back to the first place. Once again, Spirit's words ruled.

Weaving through the crowd at the Bull and Bear, I spotted one empty chair at the bar. Was it luck?

Glass of chardonnay? Check. Journal and pen? Check. I was a happy camper.

In between spurts of mental rambling on paper, I looked around the room and eyed the crowd. Standing next to me were ladies dressed to the nine's. After chatting with one of them, I learned that they were eagerly awaiting the arrival of their students so that they could begin their duties as chaperons of the senior prom.

Sitting behind me was a table of businessmen.

The crowd thinned out. The ladies left for the prom. My hand hurt from writing. The glass in front of me was empty. And more importantly, my stomach now growled like a lion.

"Check, please."

I swiveled around, hopped off my stool, and moved toward the door when I again noticed the table of businessmen. My eyes were directed to look at one gentleman in particular, and as my gaze settled on his face, my feet froze in place.

When I looked into the man's face, I saw someone who was carrying a lot of weight, both physically and emotionally. Being the health nut that I am, my mind flashed on the thought of how extra pounds could be making it difficult for his heart to function at its best. But what really gave me pause was the overwhelming feeling that this man's heart was also carrying an enormous emotional burden as well.

Spirit quickly interrupted my thought stream.

Tell him.

My feet wouldn't move. I just stood there in front of his table.

Just tell him, repeated Spirit.

Knowing better than to disregard these words, I approached the man. *Why on Earth am I doing this?*

"Excuse me," I said to this particular gentleman. "Can I speak to you over here?"

The gentleman immediately rose from his chair and followed me a few steps away. He looked puzzled yet prepared to listen to whatever I had to say.

The intensity of the moment drowned out the noise of the bar.

With a deep breath, I began.

"I know this may sound strange, but I was told to tell you something."

"OK," he replied.

Another deep breath. Here goes.

"I was told to tell you to stop killing yourself," I said and braced myself for his reaction.

The gentleman lowered his eyes to the ground.

"I know this sounds crazy, but does what I've said make any sense to you?" I asked.

With closed eyes, he slowly nodded.

"Well," I hesitated, "that's all. I was just supposed to tell you that." I smiled and began to walk away.

"Wait, wait. Have a drink with us," the gentleman urged.

"Oh, no. Thank you. But that's not what this was about," I said, hoping that he didn't think this was some cheesy pickup line or something.

"No, you must."

So I did. The gentleman, Richard, introduced me to his two friends at the table as I took my chair.

Richard and I sat in silence for a time, taking stock of what had transpired. I know I was still stunned by what just took place. God only knows what was going through Richard's head.

What *did* just take place? Why had I been told to deliver that message to him? Who told me to do it? And how in the heck did I have the courage to approach a stranger with such an odd request?

I mean, really. Had Richard taken offense to the message, I knew he could have squashed me with his pinky and swatted me away like a fly. But the oddest thing of all is that I knew he wouldn't react badly because the message I delivered was sent with love. Yes, sent with love.

What did this all mean?

Our drinks arrived, and Richard broke the silence.

"Why are you in New York?" he asked.

I told him of my book and about dedicating one of its chapters to the city's firefighters. I described how I reached the firehouse in the neighborhood, only to be told "we can't talk to you."

"And they really said they couldn't talk to you?" he asked.

"Yes, but that's OK. I knew beforehand that I would have to make the chapter on the neighborhood, rather than just firefighters ..." My words trailed off.

I looked across the table at one of Richard's friends and noticed his ear-to-ear smirk. He then cocked his head in Richard's direction.

Again Richard asked, "You mean you didn't get any firefighters?"

"No."

His friend now grinned even bigger. I looked at Richard as if to say, "What's going on?"

At this point, Richard was also wearing a sheepish grin and couldn't hold back any longer.

"I'm a retired fire captain," he said.

"No!" I drawled.

Could I believe what I was hearing? But of course this was happening. Why was I surprised? As I listened to his many wonderful achievements, I could only say *Thank you, God.*

He fired off his resume with pride, "From 1988 to 1989, I was a lieutenants representative and financial secretary of the Uniformed Fire Officers Association. And 1989–90 I was a lieutenant and president of the UFOA. And in '90, I was promoted to captain.

"And between '90 and '97, president (UFOA) and captains rep," he beamed.

He stopped midsteam and looked at me with a grin. "I can get you any firefighter you want!"

Jackpot!

Time seemed to stand still as I listened to him rattle off his resume. I didn't know if I would start laughing with joy or crying with unfathomable gratitude to Spirit for leading me to this gentleman. I did a bit of both while I listened to one of his 9/11 stories. I could barely speak.

After a quick exchange of e-mails, I headed for the door.

"I am so going to, lovingly and respectfully, use and abuse you for your connections," I said with a grin, and he returned a knowing nod.

A few days after I returned home, Richard and I spoke on the phone. I don't think either of us knew exactly how to approach the subject of how we met, or more accurately, the reason we were meant to meet. But we managed. I still giggle when I recall the first of many questions Richard asked, "are you some psychic or medium?" However, this question did set the tone for our conversation and further opened the discussion to our philosophies of life and how certain aspects of our respective beliefs were shared by some of his friends lost during 9/11.

Richard and I continue to speak to this day.

Richard Brower

> Who really knows what it is. Life is to be lived, then we will figure it out. Good or indifferent, live it. Rejoice in it and enjoy it. It only goes around once!

The Last Ripple?

I floated back to my hotel on one big giggle cloud. The joy I felt was indescribable, and the connection I now felt with Spirit was humbling. *Thank you, God, for helping me keep open my heart, mind, and ears to your Word.*

With a 5:00 AM wake-up call for my flight home, the ending to my last night in the city consisted of room service, a movie, and an early lights out.

With dinner ordered, bags packed, and the movie about to begin, I was a happy camper. All I needed was my food to arrive.

Seconds away from reaching for the phone to call after my food, I heard a knock on the door. Unfortunately, when the server lifted the plate cover, the dinner was not quite what I had ordered.

"Oh, I am so sorry," the server replied.

"Well, that's OK." I was too hungry to argue, and it was close enough.

"Well, I am afraid that if I placed your order again, it would take about an hour to arrive," he pleaded.

"Oh, no. This will do just fine."

"I tell you what," he added, "because your dinner was late, and we got it wrong, your dinner is on us!"

Déjà vu?

He continued, "And I'm going to bring you a glass of wine. On me."

Katrina ... A Terrible Lady

Although I have lived away from southern Louisiana for well over twenty years, my heart and soul remain firmly rooted in that region. When I saw the pictures of New Orleans and the Gulf Coast in the aftermath of hurricanes Katrina and Rita, my heart broke and I cried for days, and still do. The images on TV made me feel like I was watching a good friend drown right in front of me, unable to save her. I knew in my heart that the best way to heal my pain was to reach out and help people who truly suffered from this catastrophe.

After Katrina, there was no question in my mind that I would dedicate a chapter of my book to honoring the courage and determination of the survivors. I've always believed that one person can make a difference, and my hope is that my dedication will remind people that recovery efforts still need your help.

But first things first. To be able to dedicate a chapter on Katrina, I had to take a trip home to Louisiana. It had only been a few months since I spoke with survivors in New York City and based on that experience, I was very excited to have another opportunity to have my life blessed by more survivors.

At the time of Katrina (August 2005), I had just started working at my new job. Since I did not have vacation time, I couldn't physically donate my time to the recovery effort; the best I could do was to write a check. But as soon as the opportunity presented itself, I immediately booked a flight home to begin my chapter.

"Coincidentally," the timing of this trip aligned with the one-year anniversary of the hurricane.

During my visit home, I discussed with my family my plans to visit the neighborhoods affected by the hurricane. However, the more I spoke about seeing the devastation with my own eyes, the more I resisted the idea. I knew that I was just not up to it. It's odd because for as much as I wanted to go, I equally felt that it was not the thing to do.

It's OK that you're not going there. Although Spirit's words helped me feel "forgiven" for not going, in my mind I thought that I was failing my mission. It was like I was breaking a promise to Katrina survivors.

Witnessing my struggle, my family offered another option. Oprah's Angel Network (through Habitat for Humanity) was building houses for Katrina survivors somewhere in my hometown. Now, normally, you would just have to mention Oprah's name and I would be there in a heartbeat. But for some reason, Spirit told me not to pursue this lead.

Talk about being confused! I simply didn't understand what was going on with me. Why didn't I want to drive into New Orleans? And why didn't Spirit want me to check out the site of the Angel Network project?

Every move I made seemed to be working against my main goal. Once again, though, I knew not to question Spirit's direction. I simply followed.

So, without speaking to any survivors, I flew back to California. Empty handed.

But guess what? Not two weeks later, I sat in front of the TV and watched Jon Bon Jovi on *Oprah* dedicate houses to Katrina survivors. A year prior, Jon and his band donated one million dollars to Oprah's Angel Network. Now, a year later, twenty-eight homes were ready for families to move in, hence, the house dedication on *Oprah*.

And guess where the Bon Jovi house dedication was taking place? Yep, in my hometown of Houma, Louisiana. Coincidence?

I watched the show in amazement. In that moment, all of my dots were being connected. I received answers to my questions. Now I understood why I didn't have to drive into New Orleans and see the devastation firsthand. Spirit knew the reason all along.

Something else came together for me ... a full-circle connection had been made in that moment.

How perfect is it to have the last chapter of my book tied to an Oprah *episode.* The inspiration for my book started with an *Oprah* show and now, four years later, the closing chapter was helped along by yet another. I just love how that aligned.

Just a few weeks after my first trip home, I was on a plane heading back to Louisiana. However, one unanswered question continued to bug me: why had I been "told" not to visit the Angel Network project during my first trip?

The answer to this question was unknowingly provided by one of the residents of Bon Jovi Boulevard.

It felt so very odd walking up and down the street and knocking on everyone's door saying, "Hi, my name is Louise and I'm writing a book...." The words still sounded strange to me, but I became more comfortable wearing them as the day wore on, especially after repeating them about twenty times.

Each time the door opened and I spouted these words, the residents greeted me with warmth and hospitality and always kindly invited me into their homes.

Sylvia Phillips

> Life is doing things God's way. We were put on Earth for a purpose. Not our way, but God's way. We must take life as it was given to us and make it with what is given to us, be it rags or riches. Life is helping each other through love and kindness. Life is a test of trials and tribulations, and if we don't pass it, we must

take it over. We are all a ship passing through; enjoy the ride while we are here.

Angel Xochihua

The meaning of life is God. There is no other meaning. God gave us all life for a reason. He wants us to spend life the best we can. He wants us to have the best life the way He once had. Life is very valuable to us; we should spend it wisely. We should want to live life as God intended us to. People should appreciate life more because once it's gone, we can't get it back, unless we make it to Heaven.

Charlene Xochihua

The meaning of life to me means to thank God for being here, not taking life for granted. Instead of being on the streets selling drugs, drinking, being a prostitute, etc., love life and give God the glory for not being dead. If only more people would take time out of their busy schedules and praise God and give him thanks for being here, it would make their lives much easier.

Patrick Trosclair

To me, the meaning of life is basic survival. That means to accomplish things that normally you don't do, things like finding shelter during or after a storm, having food when none is available, and keeping your family safe from harm.

Paula Buquet

God gave us life to live, love, and care for one another and to be a servant for His kingdom. Some He gave children to raise, to care for and nurture. He blessed us with special gifts to give the gift of life.

Miss Paula answered the door with a welcoming smile; however, she was a bit leery about speaking to me. She took the time to explain that when residents learned that their houses were a part of the Bon Jovi/ Oprah's Angel Network program, they were not allowed to talk to anyone about it until after the official presentation on *Oprah*. Now that the show had already aired, the restriction was no longer in effect.

In an instant, I knew Miss Paula's explanation had answered the question that was still lingering in my mind: why had I not visited the Angel Network project during my first visit to my hometown? I now understood that had I not listened to Spirit and approached the residents at that time, they would not have spoken to me.

As I listened to Miss Paula's stories, I couldn't help but smile knowing that Spirit had known the reason all along. *You're exactly where you're supposed to be.*

Dorothy Hampton

The meaning of life is to move on. Deal the hand that's been dealt you. I struggle with other families.

I lived in a FEMA trailer for nine months. God gave me another chance at my age. I feel truly blessed. I thank everybody that has helped with this recovery, especially Habitat for Humanity, partner families, Oprah, and Bon Jovi. Most of all, I thank God.

Barbara Frankle

Life to me is precious. Everyone should enjoy each day like it's your last and always put God first.

I've been truly blessed after being affected by Katrina and Rita. The Lord has blessed me and my family with a beautiful Habitat home. So again, remember to always put God first.

Essence Bridges

> Life is like joy to me. It makes you want to be happy to be awake in the morning and to see and greet people, laugh, hug, kiss, talk, walk and run, and also to bring more life into the world. It is just a blessing to have life.

Wesley Jones

> I never knew how good life would be until Katrina. Then (after Katrina), I found out I had lung cancer. Right now, I try to live day by day and I ask God to spare my life a bit longer because I know there's no cure for lung cancer.
>
> I brushed hard with death, got cancer, and took chemotherapy. Each morning, it's just so good to be alive that my heart is overwhelmed, and I cry. I'm so glad to see another day.
>
> I'm trying to put life into perspective; words cannot express it. Only the supreme ruler understands what life means to me. I look back on my life and ask myself if I could do it over. I would not smoke.
>
> I have been blessed through God. But no one knows how it feels to be a victim of such a situation until it falls upon you. I'm a fighter, through the grace of God. I go to bed, and I don't worry. I wake up and don't worry. But I do appreciate every day.
>
> This brings me closer to God. I try to live a good life now. I thank God that thoughts of ending my life have never crossed my mind. Life means more than anything can ever be.
>
> Most of all, I hope to reach the young children and tell them: don't smoke.

Each resident had his or her own unique story about Katrina. They told of the different places where they evacuated to weather the hurricane, the number of times they had to relocate in order to keep a roof over their heads, the struggles to just obtain food and water, and how they continued to survive the pain.

As one resident recalled, "We all just thought we would be going home when the storm was over."

They may never return home. (Take a few moments to really connect with how that would impact your life if you suffered such a tragic loss.)

As I listened to each story, I looked deep into the eyes of the storyteller. No matter how each story varied, it was in their eyes that I saw the common threads that profoundly wove these people together as a community.

Present in their eyes were the strong threads of pain, confusion, and heartbreak caused by Katrina. Gently wrapped around that core was a thick thread of amazement. All were amazed that they had survived the storm; and as importantly, all were amazed by their good fortune provided by Habitat for Humanity, Oprah's Angel Network, and Bon Jovi's donation.

The final thread—a strong, golden thread—served as a casing for the bundle of strands. This thread was one of immense gratitude. They were grateful for the hundreds of loving volunteers from across the country who helped create the safety of a lovely new home. Grateful for being alive and for being able to see it all as a blessing.

After reflecting on all that had happened to her family, one resident summed it up: "The whole picture was just blessings. Blessings. Let God do His work."

I left Bon Jovi Boulevard with conflicting feelings. On one hand, my heart was overflowing with my own deep feelings of gratitude and that of humility—gratitude for the love and generosity shown by the residents who so freely shared their time and hearts with me, and humbled by the sheer honor I felt for having spent time with each of them.

Yet on the other hand, despite all the good feelings I took away from my experience, I drove out of the neighborhood feeling just awful. Yes, awful. My heart ached over the fact that I was not a better writer. If I were, I would be able to convey the enormity of my experience. To have witnessed the amazing energy and spirit of the people living on this simple little street, in a simple little town, and not do it justice in words ... well, I hoped that the residents would forgive my shortcomings.

To this day, I cry when I relive the beautiful time I spent with the residents of Bon Jovi Boulevard. They have forever changed my heart.

Now It's Your Turn

Now that you've read about the adventures of my new chapter, you know that it revolved around two things: listening to Spirit and living with one simple question.

Although I plan to live with the meaning of life question for some time, I want to offer this question to you so that your own adventure can begin. If you accept, here is what I ask of you:

First, use your finger as a marker for this page and then grab a pen or pencil. Next, sit in a quiet place where you will not be disturbed. Now, ask yourself the question aloud: What is the meaning of life?

Breathe in the question, and let your thoughts gently form in your mind. Take only a few minutes to collect your thoughts, and then begin to write the first thing that comes to mind. Let your words flow freely onto the page. Do not stop the flow by editing your words or making several drafts of your answer. Simply capture your spontaneous answer.

Stop writing when what is in your heart is on the paper.

Lastly, do not judge or criticize your answer. Embrace the fact that what you have written is simply a reflection of one particular spontaneous moment in your life. Let it be.

Here is another idea for you: do this same exercise on your next five birthdays. (For some reason, we tend to question life on our birthdays.) On every birthday, ask yourself the question and write your spontaneous answer. Then put it away. At the end of five years, take them out and read them. You will be amazed (and entertained) when you compare your answers over time.

Yet another idea is to select a few members of your family or friends and ask them the question on each of their next five birthdays. At the end of the fifth year, present to them a gift of their answers. You will be giving them one of the best gifts ever.

I leave you now with one request: Start listening to Spirit. Right now, at this very moment, He is telling you how to fill the spontaneous moments of *your* life with meaning. All you have to do is listen.

Birthday Answer #1

Birthday Answer #2

Birthday Answer #3

Birthday Answer #4

Birthday Answer #5

978-0-595-42971-4
0-595-42971-8

Printed in the United States
)6LV00002B/52-132/A